THE
WORD
There Is No Other Way

The WORD - There Is No Other Way
Copyright © 2018 Tamiko Powell

Powell Publishing

All rights reserved. No part of this book may be reproduced (except for inclusion in reviews), disseminated or utilized in any form or by any means, electronic or mechanical, including photocopying, recording, or in any information storage and retrieval system, or the Internet/World Wide Web without written permission from the author or publisher.

Book design by:
Arbor Services, Inc.
www.arborservices.co/

Printed in the United States of America

The WORD - There Is No Other Way
Tamiko Powell

1. Title 2. Author 3. Memoir

Library of Congress Control Number: 2017918805
ISBN 13: 978-0-692-98851-0

THE WORD
There Is No Other Way

TAMIKO POWELL

*This book is dedicated to
My Lord and Savior.*

Contents

Chapter 1
My Shoes *1*

Chapter 2
True Love *9*

Chapter 3
The Goat *13*

Chapter 4
Not Again *23*

Chapter 5
Where Were You *35*

Chapter 6
How Could You? *55*

Chapter 7
No Apology *59*

Chapter 8
I Wish It Would Stop *69*

Chapter 9
Almost Famous *77*

Chapter 10
The Idiot *105*

Chapter 11
The Legal Thief *127*

Chapter 12
Silver Coins *133*

Chapter 13
The Demon *145*

Chapter 14
The Awakening *163*

Foreward

Everyone has a story, and in order for people to listen to me, they have to connect to me. I'm showing the things that have happened to me. I want readers to know that God is alive, He's watching, He sees, and He knows.

This Is Not
A Game, People

No,
You Will Not
Get Rid of Me
Nor Shut Me Up

His Word
Will Be Heard
And Honored
Through Me
I Am
The Chosen One

It's Time to Fight Back
What Are You Afraid Of?

The Devil Whispers
And Delivers
As You Run, Jump
To His Beck and Call

He Has Played Me
Many Times
And As I've Learned
There's a Little Bit of Truth
In Every Lie
Now It's On

The System
Has You Strapped
And Chained
Frightened
To Wit's End

Surviving, Fitting In
Living in Sin
But You Have to Know
This World
Is Coming to an End

You Have Two Choices
It's Either
Up or Down

What Are You Gonna Do
When There's
No Place to Run

These High Prices
And Cheap Thrills
Are the Definition Of
A Sorry, Sad Tomorrow

Hiding
Is Out of the Question
You Will Give
An Account
For What You've Done

Know
That He Is Real
Come As Children
And Believe
Without Seeing

You Will Hear
The Blowing Horns
Winning the Battle
Look
For the White Horse
Riding the King of Kings
Holding
The Two-Headed Sword

The Sight of the Beginning
Of a New Tomorrow

Do You Believe?
Are You Curious?
Eyes All on Him
Follow Him

Survival As He Rides
He Gives Us Peace
In His Promise
Of Our Afterlife

There Is No More Time
Like the First Time
As He Came Here
To Tell Us
To Believe in Him

We Walk in Disrespect
Of Desperation
Living Dirty
As We Run
A Life of Disgrace
For Our Own Personal
Satisfaction

This Time
Is a Different Story
In This Time
You Must
Run to Him

Once Again
Are You Curious?
Do You Believe?

Rise Up
The Ones That Do
And Learn
That Believing in Him
Pays Off

No More
Unhappiness

The Misleading Lies
The Devil Expresses
Worry, Confusion, Depression,
And Stress
Will Now Be Forgotten
Along with Your Past

Do You Believe?

Chapter 1

My Shoes

It was an ordinary Monday. I was wearing my green plaid uniform, the standard attire for St. Paschal's Catholic School in Oakland, California. I had chosen the dress with the white button-down shirt underneath. Some days I wore the skirt instead. Boys had to wear brown corduroy pants with white shirts, while the girls had the option of skirts or dresses. Today I wanted to look especially nice because I had brand-new socks and shoes that I couldn't wait to wear. My beautiful black patent leather Mary Janes were waiting for me. I ran to ask my mother if I could wear them instead of my usual shoes. Her first response was a firm no. Being the stubborn little seven-year-old I was, I continued pestering her until I got what I wanted. I slipped my socks on and then slid my feet into my shiny new shoes, excited to show them off to all my friends.

    I arrived at school with my sister and brother and then went to Mrs. Hart's class. We said the pledge of allegiance, then were ushered into the gymnasium to have dance class with Mrs. Washburn. I was brimming with excitement about my new shoes as we walked onto the gleaming wooden floor and stood in a C shape. Mrs. Washburn was waiting for us and began taking attendance as we stood in formation. When she got to me, she looked down at my shoes.

"Tamiko, this floor was just shellacked and buffed. You can either take off your shoes and dance in your socks or go sit down."

I looked down at my shoes and then around at the rest of the class. They were all wearing shoes, although none were as crisp and new as mine. I recalled the events of the day before, when after Sunday mass was finished, the priest and altar boys walked down the aisle and through the giant doors that led from the chapel to the gymnasium. The congregation followed. As we entered the gymnasium, we were greeted by women holding napkins and offering us coffee, tea, juice, and an assortment of delicious cookies and treats.

The day before was like every other Sunday. We always spent time in the gymnasium, milling about and socializing after mass. And yesterday, like every other Sunday, my mother, my auntie, and at least fifty other men and women had walked on that floor with their high heels and special Sunday shoes. There were even other children wearing Mary Janes. All of this swirled through my head as I stood contemplating Mrs. Washburn's ultimatum.

I couldn't understand why I wasn't allowed to wear my shoes on the floor when the day before, so many other people had trounced through with no care whatsoever. But rather than argue with my teacher, I decided to answer her politely. I looked at the rest of the class, then at my teacher.

"I will go sit down," I said.

This response elicited a gasp of "ooohs" and "oh, she told you" utterances from the other plaid- and corduroy-wearing students. They giggled and snickered as if I had in some way defied Mrs. Washburn.

But all I had done was exactly what she had suggested. I had opted to sit out of class.

Apparently, Mrs. Washburn didn't like my response or the reaction from the students. As I started to walk away from the students to the chairs lining the wall, Mrs. Washburn walked up behind me and snatched me by the arm. "Come with me," she said in a harsh tone.

Moments later we were in the principal's office. I couldn't believe what was happening. My little seven-year-old mind was swirling with confusion. Hadn't I done what she asked? Hadn't I followed the rules? She had told me I had a choice. I chose to sit out of class. And I had answered her in a respectful way.

As I sat there and tried to figure out exactly what was happening, Mrs. Washburn took out a bar of Zest soap. I looked wide eyed at her and at the principal standing next to her. Then I opened my mouth and screamed. *This woman has lost her mind*, I thought. Why was I being punished for doing the right thing? Why was I in the principal's office about to have a bar of soap shoved in my mouth?

She told me to open my mouth.

"I'm gonna call my daddy!" I screamed. I hollered to the secretary sitting outside the principal's office. "Call my sister and brother! They go to this school! Get them down here!"

Moments later, my sister and brother came running up. I was still screaming. Finally, the secretary got my father on the phone. He asked the principal what I had done wrong, and the principal told him that I had been talking badly. Then my father asked to speak to me. The principal handed me the phone and my father asked me what happened. I told him that I hadn't been talking badly.

He said, "Tell me what happened."

I explained to my father that I had done exactly what the teacher had asked. My father told me to give the phone back to the principal. I handed it back, and my father told the principal that he wasn't to lay a finger on me. Before I knew it, the soap was put away and the principal, Mrs. Washburn, and the secretary dismissed me and my siblings back to class.

Now, I believe in principles. I believe in doing the right thing. But I know that I didn't do anything wrong that day. I think the only reason I got punished is because Mrs. Washburn's pride got hurt. She was, after all, the teacher. She was probably upset because a whole class of first graders was laughing at her. But why should I have been punished for that? I shouldn't have. The whole experience confused me. I had been about to be punished for doing nothing wrong.

This story introduced me to my honesty and authenticity as a child of God. I was born and raised in that church. I was baptized in that church. It was the only church I knew. And to have a woman treat me that way in my church? A teacher? I was so confused. But that wasn't the first or the last time I was confronted by people who questioned my honesty or authenticity as a child of God.

When we left the principal's office that day, still unsure what had happened, my stomach did the willies and my hands sweated. I remember my brother was very happy. He looked down at me and said, "We're not going to take that. We won our fight."

I looked from him to my older sister. She smiled at me as we walked down the hallway back to class.

Yeah, I thought. We won our fight. I was so relieved. I felt vindicated. God was on our side.

Here Is What's Going to Happen
It Doesn't Matter
If You're Not Ready for This

All of Your Unwise Decisions
Will Re-exist

You Run to God for Forgiveness
But You Keep On Doing It

Why Is Loving the Lord
Such a Hateful Thing?
He's Hated without a Cause
Is It Because
You Don't Understand His Love?

This Up and Down Roller Coaster Ride
Is From Your Selfishness

Women and Men
Know the Rules
You Were All Given a Conscience

To What Extent of Listening
Depends On Your Willingness

From Right and Knowing Wrong to Another
Your Flesh Decides Your Free Will
On How It Wants to Stomp on Its Brethren

Humans' High Moral of Morality
Doing What's Wrong and Believing It's Right
Manipulating and Reexamining
Telling Themselves
My Wants Are What I Need
Whom I Step On
I Can Live With

The "Motive" for Everyday Participation
Of What's in It for Me

Day and Night
Night and Day
The Elephant's in the Room
And Your Collective Misery
Knows It

What's Yours Is Mine
And What's Mine Is Mine
I Thought You Knew This
This World We Live In
This Is How We Move in It

From the End to Beginning
Better Understood
You Judge One Another
As Though You Have a Right To

As the Piper Plays the Fiddle
The Confusion Is a Battle Field
In Your Everyday Living

We Must Observe and Help One Another
And Bow Down
Cry On Our Knees
"Father Please Help Me"
But Still You Do Not Know, My Father
Because You Do Not Know Me

How Long Do You Think This Free Will
Will Last?
Choices Are Being Made and It's Sad
You're Not Aware of It
As You Sit and Do Nothing
Your Mouth Runs Rampant
With Crap Coming Out of It
The Clock Is Ticking
Do You Care to Listen?
Or Are You Playing the Victim
Once Again

The Devil's On Us As Shadows On Prey
You've Given Your Condolences
To His Activities
Through Your Greed and Selfishness

I Kid You Not
The Devil Is Real
There Is
A Heaven and a Hell

Your Mouth and Your Actions
Are Your Enemy
And You Act As Though
You Don't
Even
Know This

Chapter 2

True Love

My favorite boutique shoe store in San Francisco had sent my friend Eduard a postcard advertisement that they were having 40% off deal. I had a few extra dollars burning a hole in my pocket. To say I was excited about this sale would be an understatement. I love my shoes and I love this store.

Around 4 00pm I grabbed my purse, slid it over my shoulder as I grabbed my keys with a quick twirl on my finger and walked out the front door of my friend's apartment. Locked the door behind me and headed to the elevator with focus, focus on shoes. "Dang this elevator is slow" as I hit the button again and again. It finally made its way to the third floor to pick me up. As I chuckled...I thought to myself. "Slowly but surely" as it gradually made its way down making some strange weird radeling sounds to the main lobby.

Doors finally opening up to a mirrored foyer "Yay! As I started heading out on my adventure. Pushing the glass doors open, walking through as I'm stepping down on the white marble steps, making a left turn passing the green ivy stepping down off of the sidewalk now walking almost in the middle of the street. It was a beautiful October day.

The weather was perfect, clear skies with a light warm breeze I felt against my skin. Smiling as I enjoyed that summer feel. It was October 17th of 1989. A day that would live in History for the Bay Area of California and a day of awaking for me. As I headed down the dead end block looking at the tree's leaves moving in the wind, I was still a ways away from where the car was parked on the left hand side. My footsteps continued my journey as I'm walking in the middle of the street looking at my car that is close and ahead of me I heard a voice saying "TAMIKO - DO NOT GO". I dismissed this voice I heard and continued towards my car. Shoes were all that was on my mind and I threw in maybe a new handbag to match. As I put the key in the car door and turned to get in, those thoughts were interrupted by a second command. The voice made its presence strongly vibrate through my body "TAMIKO - DO NOT GO".

I could not ignore it this time. I stopped what I was doing and looked around not seeing anyone, ok, I thought to myself, there is something more to this, so I turned around and walked back to the apartment. As I walked in I closed the door and locked it behind me. Putting my purse and keys on the coffee table, I turned around and walked to the kitchen to grab a glass of water then stepped back sitting down in the living room on the couch. Thinking to myself, the shoes will have to wait while I was taking a sip of water. The sale is for a week so I'm not missing out as I sat the glass of water down on the table. I was sitting at the end of the couch with my legs crossed and my arm resting on the arm.

I had a concern weighing heavy on my mind then speaking out loud. I asked the question "What happened outside. I was obedient and I did not go. why, why?" After asking the question I sat there in a room of silence for a few moments in wonder. Nothing was going on. Just Feeling the warm breeze through the drapes, but then my eyes became aware, startled I became...As I looked down at the coffee table I saw ripples in the water of my drinking glass then the glass moved. Then I started shaking in my seat like the couch was a roller coaster and I didn't have a safety bar. Scared, nervous.

Next I knew it felt like it was getting worse. Stronger! As I was sitting there not knowing what to do...What do I do I thought!? But I was too scared to move. Looking around as I saw the statues wobble, pictures moving falling to the floor. Car alarms started going off as I listened through the opened sliding glass window. 5:04pm the Loma Prieta earthquake hit the Bay Area. One of the most devastating earthquakes in California History with the tragic loss of lives for those who were traveling on the same freeway I would have used. If I didn't stop and listen I would have been one of them. If I ignored what I was being told, I would have been traveling at that exact same time. It was not my time to die so "The Almighty" stopped me. *Oh I am grateful ! Thank you "Almighty" for loving me!*

Chapter 3

The Goat

We lived in the hills of Oakland, California, and had a lot of animals growing up. All the properties in our neighborhood were good sized, at least a half acre. We had an acre to an acre and a half of prime property at the top of a hill overlooking the valley. At night, we could see the beautiful sight of all the lights of the valley twinkling below. Because we had such a large property, we had plenty of room for animals. I grew up with dogs, cats, horses, a rooster, and even chickens. My father had gotten the chickens so we could get eggs from them. We built a chicken house and waited for the chickens to produce. They never did.

We loved all of our animals. But our neighbors weren't big fans. Our chickens were loud and our rooster liked to crow. We got complaints that our rooster crowed every day. But he was a broken rooster. He would crow during the day but never early in the morning.

We had a police officer come out to check that we were within the law. Because of the distance between the properties, we had plenty of space to keep our animals. In fact, the officer said that all of our animals were being kept within our property limits and we were well within our rights to have them all. We did, however, eventually move the chicken house down to the stable so the neighbors wouldn't hear them so much. But that didn't prevent someone from coming in and killing them all one day.

People can be so cruel. Our Father (God) told me that He does not like the way people abuse the animals. The killing of the chickens was just one example that must have broken our Father's heart.

Then there was our goat, Tilly. We got the goat when I was in elementary school. My dad brought her home because he couldn't let the horses out to graze without risking them hopping the fence. The goat was a small animal who could graze at the back of property. The moment I saw Tilly, I fell in love. She was all white, about the size of a standard poodle, with coarse fur and two tiny little horns. She was the cutest little thing. I played with her all the time, and she would follow me around like a puppy. Our property was large enough that I never had to put her on a leash. One time, she followed me into the house, just baa, baa-ing away. I loved that goat so much.

Our property was a cut-through for the neighborhood kids to get to other parts of the neighborhood. Even after my father put a board up to keep our horses from grazing off our property, that didn't stop the kids. They would bend down and go under that board and then up the trail that we walked our horses on.

One day, a tall, skinny black kid walked straight up the hill on our property on the trail that passes the stables. I yelled at him to get off our property, but he kept walking. From where I stood at the top of the hill, you could make a right and walk over the patio into our house or go left straight past the apple tree by my parents' bedroom window. I yelled at him again to get off our property, but he just kept walking. He walked past the apple tree, right by my parents' bedroom, and glanced toward the windows. He knew I saw him looking because he yelled my name. I said, "Look, I don't know you. You need to get off my property! You don't belong here." He finally left and went off to one of the streets. I didn't have any idea who he was or how he knew who I was.

Even though he knew my name, I didn't feel scared. I was close to our back patio door, and my dog was with me. My brother and sister were home, too. No matter what this kid in the jeans and denim jacket did, I knew I could get away. I knew I would be safe. He kept walking, looking back at me as he disappeared down the back of our property and out of sight. He eventually disappeared down the street.

The next day, my brother ran from the stables and screamed that our goat was dead. I flew out of the house and ran down the hill in the back of our yard to see for myself. There, about fifty feet from the stables, by the fence, lay Tilly. My beautiful, harmless, sweet, white goat lay on the grass with her throat slit. I couldn't believe what I saw. Why? Why would someone kill such a sweet, innocent animal? Tilly never harmed anyone! All she did was eat, graze, play, and baa. What type of fool would hurt an animal that hadn't done anything wrong? I could never be sure, but I thought maybe she was killed by the boy that had been on our property the day before.

That experience hurt me badly and really got under my skin. I carry the baggage of that memory to this day. When I see someone hurting an animal of any kind, I am deeply bothered. When I see the ads with dogs in cramped cages, not being fed, I am overwhelmed with sorrow.

As an adult, I used to go running in the state park behind my house. One day, when I was on my way back from a run, I heard a whining noise. I didn't know what it was. As I continued to run I realized I was getting closer to the whining sound, which got louder as I drew nearer.

As I came around a corner, I saw a man with his dog. I picked up a stick and was about to go after the man. He looked up at me and held out his hands as he stuttered, trying to get a word out. An older woman was with him and she called out that the dog was a whiner. She said it loudly so I would know nothing bad was going on with the dog. I'm glad that was all it was. Because if I had caught that man abusing that animal, I don't know what I would have done!

To this day, I have a special spot in my heart for animals. I believe what our Father (God) told me. We should never abuse our animals. We should treat all animals and people kindly. Today I have my own pets that I care for. I adopted them all. I have two black cats and two bunnies. I was told by the lady I got them from to not let them out around Halloween. People are afraid of black cats and will do horrible things to them that time of year.

One of my bunnies is black, too. She couldn't get a home because nobody wanted a black bunny. I saw her and immediately fell in love. She is my Duchess, my Tinky Binky. My other bunny's name is Sir Blaze. My cat's names are Peanut and Karrot. When I took my little kitten to her first checkup with the veterinarian, he thought I had gone a little far calling her Karrot. Then I explained that I had named her Karrot because she's like a little piece of gold. The doctor smiled. "Oh, I get it." He understood.

That's how I see all of my animals. And I think that's the way our Father wants us to see them all—as the precious gems that they are. I only wish that people would treat all animals well, feed them properly, and not smoke in front of them. It kills them! Their little bodies can only take so much.

Everyone On
Planet Earth
Has Heard My Name
One Way or Another
You Throw It Around
Foul Mouth, Slang
Fashion Gratification

That Shows Me
No Respect
Nor Honor

These Lies
Keep You in Bondage
Games That You Play

Jealousies, Sins
You Treat
One Another In
Inhumane Ways
That Hold You Down

What Makes You Think
You're Better
Than Your Brethren?
The Past to You
Is the Past
All Is Forgotten

Your Actions Show
You Care Not to Remember,
What You've Been Told

But Still
You Are My Children

With the Possibilities
That You Still
Can Behold

There Is No Purpose of Sin
It's the Flesh
Doing You Wrong

In the End
The Choice Is Yours
Glory or Fire

You Must Be Aware
As Your Days Grow Old
My Word
Never Changes

It's Been the Same Way
Since My Son
Walked the Earth

Examples
Of What to Do
And Not to Do
In Perfection of Making You

You Are All
Images of Me
Cut from a Cloth
Separately

Not Composed
As a Puppet
Your Free Will
Overrode My Wisdom,
Perfection
But to Love Me
Freely
And to Love
One Another

Your Mind Battles
Feelings
That Should Not
Be Given a Chance
To Vote
Is Where
You Need to Learn
Self-Control

This Place
Of Decisions
Where You
Educate Yourself
To Understand
How to Control
The Flesh

To Keep
From Ruin,
Decay
And Destruction
There IS NO Other Way

Reap From the Spirit
Life and Life Eternal
As John 10:10 Has Stated

Know That Our Father
Is Coming Soon

Show Convictions
Of Strong Integrity
Believing in Him

Chapter 4

Not Again

These are the petty things that people concern themselves with that don't even matter.

I was walking to my kitchen to start my day one morning, and the phone rang. It was unusual for me to get a phone call so early. Most of my friends and family know my routine. I feed my cats and rabbits, let the cats out to play, set up the rabbits' play area in the backyard, let them go out to go crazy, and then I get my coffee. That's a little too much to do and talk on the phone at the same time.

On the phone was Kelly, my chiropractor's wife. We exchanged greetings. I was expecting that maybe she was about to change my appointment for later that afternoon, which had happened a couple of times before.

"I was curious," Kelly said.

I waited. I've found in the past that this phrase always precedes something negative. Maybe it's because people always say curiosity killed the cat.

"So, I wanted to know," Kelly said, "are you just like Obama, both African American and white?"

"Do I look like Obama?" I said.

"Um, no," Kelly replied.

"Let me tell you. If you go around asking people that, you might end up with a hand in your face; it's rude," I told her. "And girlfriend, if I did tell you, would it do anything for you? Would it pay your rent, would it send your kids to college?"

"No," she said. "Oh, I feel really stupid."

"Well, my grandmother used to tell me, think before you speak." She didn't know what to say. "Oh, yeah."

"All right," I told her. "I'll be in for my appointment at two o'clock."

I Am Love in Every Definition of the Word
I Am Full of Peace in My Way of Living

I Forgive and Forget
I Give Grace with Sincerity of Your Mistakes
Trying to Love Me

I Offer Tranquility
And Everlasting Life
If You Follow and Believe in Me

I Have Placed a Woman and a Man
Two of My Children
To Be Respected the Same Way

You Were Given Gifts
To Take Care of One Another
For Survival to Live On and On

The Love I Ask of You to Give to Your Neighbor
Equals Peace and Harmony

To Believe in Me without Seeing
To Know Me As Though You Have

But You Wish to Disgrace My Name
With Abomination of My Word

Disgust Is What You Do to Me
And Believe That It Is Right to Do So

My Word Is Falling Apart
My Son Has Suffered and Died for You

Behind Your Inappropriate Maniacal Hate
That You Continue Every Day to Do

All I Have Done for You
You Wish to Not See

Through the Miracles
I Have Given Each and Every One of You
With No Appreciation

I Am the Beginning and the End
That Your Ignorance Refuses to Understand
I Am the Alpha and the Omega
That You Hate without a Cause
Refusing to Know Me

You Fight Me with Chaos
Laws Written in Your Laws
That Must Be Believed
And Fulfilled

A Servant Is Never Greater
Than His Master
But You Feel
You Can
Get Rid of Me

Your Time Is of the Essence
But Your Continuance
To Manipulate and Challenge
The Innocent
Is Inappropriate
From the Way I Hoped
It Would Be

Here We Go Again
With the Same Old Decisions

Worried About Me, Me, Me, Me, Me

I'm Trying to Find It
Where Can It Be
The Thing That Will Make Me Happy

But I'm Trying to Learn to Forget My Past
To Change My Mental Well-being for Better Things

I'm Tired of Eating My Words
This Diet Is Making Me Sick
It'll Probably Kill Me
If I Don't Get Saved Quick

Where, Where, Oh Where Can I Find
The Words to Heal Me

This Disruptive Cycle
Of Selfishness and Greed
That Surrounds Me

Again and Again

This Little Blue Ball
That I Run Around On
I Can't Breathe

I've Learned to Finally See
I've Surrendered and Now I Bow Down to Thee
The Learning and Understanding of the Nine Things
The Lord Has Been Trying to Tell Me

Love Brings Joy
Joy Is Peace
Patience Is Understanding
Kindness Brings Goodness You Can See
Faithfulness Is Strength
Gentleness Brings You Back to Love, Joy, and Peace
Self-control Is Patience
Where Nothing Is Lacking in These Nine Things

Is Where You Are Free!

Are You Afraid to Die?
You Have Regrets
That You Did
That You Can't Deny

Are Those Evil Things
Haunting You?

That Time of Consummating
Your Actions
Now Getting the Best of You?

You Knew It Was Wrong
When You Did It
You Knew Your Last Day
Was Coming
When It Begins
You Will Pay for It

As Our Father
Who Art in Heaven
Stated
In His Will and Testament
Don't Act Like You Don't Know
You Will Reap What You Sow

On Your Last Breath
It Will Not Be Delayed
It's Your Judgment Day

Society Teaches You
How to Be Cruel
Your Flesh Stands Tall
In Decisions about You

There Are No Excuses
For the Things
That You Do

Do Unto Others
As You Would Have Them
Do Unto You

Why Is Understanding of This
So Hard for You
But Yet
You Don't Like Ugly
When It's Done Back to You

We Are All
Walking This Earth
Fighting Pretty Much
For the Same Thing

Love, Peace, and Prosperity
Dealing with Democracy
And the Ugliness
We Have Made

Not Believing
The Devil Is Real
He's Out to Get Us
Realize This

Look Around
The Selfishness and Greed
Is a Serious Thing
Stop Using Our Father's
Name in Vain

The Disrespect
We Continue to Do
As We Hurt One Another
Hurts Our Father

All He Asks
Is That We Respect
One Another
Control Your Emotions
And Think Twice
About Your Reaction

You Play These Games
As You Lie, You Cheat, and You Steal

But You Get Upgrades in Life
That Show How Well
You Do It

Just to Let You Know
It Was Never Yours
In the Beginning
And You Can't
Take It with You

Everyone Is the Same
He Who Has No Sins
Be the First to Throw
The Stone

We Were All Born
Then Die

Ashes to Ashes
Dust to Dust
What Gives You
The Right to Judge?

A Gossip Mouth
Can't Retract Its Sins
Again Rethink

Think Before You Speak
Stupidity and Ignorance
Is Not Something
You Want to Embellish

In This World
The Word
Is the Most Important Thing
Learn It
Know It
And Live It
'Cause Once Again
Jesus Is On His Way!

Chapter 5

Where Were You

Oakland, CA, on July 1, 1991, is the day that changed my life forever. And I don't remember most of it.

I can tell you how it started. I was at a car wash and happened to see my cousin, Carlos. We struck up a conversation . . . he mentioned something about having a new motorcycle, and he offered me a ride on it around the block. Once we got to his place, I waited outside while he retrieved his keys from the house.

Now, it had been years since I had seen him, but for whatever reason, he talked me into taking a ride with him on his bike. It never occurred to me not to trust him. Honestly, I didn't know him well enough to gauge that there might be anything off about his behavior. I didn't realize at the time that he was a functioning alcoholic and drug addict. I only have other people's stories to piece together what happened to me. If I had thought anything was wrong with him, I would never have gotten on the bike. As it turned out, he was able to walk away from the accident. I never saw him again.

In the police report, the officer said the driver, Carlos, lost control of the bike coming around the corner when he gave it too much power. I flew a hundred feet off the backseat like a person being blown out of a cannon, and came straight down on my head. Then the bike flipped over and landed on me. I slid on the concrete and rocks, which is how I ended up with road rash down my body and face.

Many people witnessed the accident, which happened in front of a motel and a liquor/convenience store, and ran over to help. A policeman was just coming out of the convenience store when it happened. When the paramedics arrived, they cut me out of my clothes, did what they could for my injuries, and took me to the emergency room at Highland Hospital. People told me later that my cousin pretended not to know who I was and said I tried to steal the bike from him. We are first cousins; our mothers are sisters. The bike belonged to his brother, Michael, and I guess Carlos felt like he needed to come up with some kind of explanation. Of course, I'm pretty sure that lie was revealed soon enough.

My next memory was waking up in the hospital.

It's hard to explain to someone what it's like to wake up from a coma. You're in one place, and then suddenly you wake up in another place you don't recognize. Since you don't know how you got there, you try to fill in the spaces between. Maybe you were kidnapped. Maybe these people in white are out to get you. Shapes and objects that you could easily name don't have the same meaning they did before. Words come out sometimes but often aren't the right words, or they are in a completely wrong order. You feel like you just woke up from a dream, only you can't remember the middle, the end, or the point of any of it. People who you should know seem like strangers. You can't understand why they're around or pretending to know you because you certainly don't know them. At times I wanted to say something but couldn't figure out how to get my point across, and then my whole idea would be gone, leaving emptiness where something else had been.

My little sister said my cousins came to the hospital just to see how messed up I was. The nurses wouldn't let my little sister in because she was underage, but they let all the cousins see me. After one of the nurses barred her from seeing me, she went in the bathroom, put on some makeup, and let her hair down. The next nurse on shift thought she looked older, so she allowed her in to see me. After that, my sister went to the front desk and asked Dr. Kaswani to only let immediate family in to see me. Dr. Kaswani agreed with her because he too felt it was too many people and it was stressing me.

My sister said when I woke up I kept saying the name Suzy. She thought it was odd because she knew Suzy wasn't one of my favorite people. I remember a few things while I was in and out of my coma. I remember my auntie saying, "You still have your pretty face." I also asked, "Did you get him, did they get him?" I guess I was referring to my cousin. My sister said after I asked this question I fell right back to sleep.

My sister had a cookbook she would bring to the hospital. She would point to recipes and say, "We used to make these." She didn't know if I would come back or not. My family had priests come and visit me. I remember looking at the steel guardrails on either side of my bed as my mind came in and out. I would be aware of things and then slowly drift away. I have a collection of hazy, disjointed memories from that time.

My sister told me she remembered Auntie Kathrine asking Father Ward from the Episcopalian Church that she attends to see me and say a prayer. My auntie also brought me a little white cross and left it on the nightstand next to my bed. I must have spoken, because Father Ward hushed me with his finger over his lips and went back to praying. I remember staring at his cassock and vestments while he said the prayer. Another time, I vaguely remember a nurse coming into my room to give me a sponge bath.

The doctor was called to my bedside because I sat up in my bed. When Doctor Kaswani arrived, I was trapped in that bed, my body broken. Eduard told me I was looking around at people, trying to figure out where I was and who these people were. I was in so much pain. It was like I had been out of my body and all of a sudden I was plunged back into it, experiencing all the aches and pains from each injury I'd suffered. The doctor said my name and then asked me what year it was. My eyes popped open and remained big and alert. I remember hearing my friend say, "Oh my gosh, she just looked at him like he lost his mind."

The doctor asked me a litany of other questions, such as, "Who is the president? What's your name? What's your birthday?" My family laughed and was excited to see me responding to the doctor. "Miki's up," they said. My friend Eduard brought me a peach, and I cleaned it like it was an apple, breathing on it and rubbing it on my shirt before taking a small bite.

I don't know if I answered Dr. Kaswani's questions correctly, but I remember that he tilted his head at me, so I probably answered incorrectly. My family said my speech was backward. The doctor told them, "Do not stress her. Do not bring in pictures, trying to make her remember things. Let her remember on her own terms."

They kept me in the ICU at Highland for a while longer before transferring me to Fairmont because I was still in a deep coma for almost a month. During that time, my sister called Social Security to set me up on disability to make sure I would be financially okay when I woke up. My sister and Eduard told me that the day the agent from Social Security came to see me in the ICU at Highland Hospital, Eduard, my sister, and mother were in the room along with my doctor and a nurse who were checking my vitals. The Social Security agent came in the room and asked if the girl lying in the bed was me and a few other questions on her checklist for clarification. Then she asked the doctor, "Is she faking it?" The doctor and my family looked at each other then at her, dumbfounded. What was she thinking, or was she not thinking at all? I laid there in a coma attached to tubes to eat, breathe, monitor my heart rate, and with catheters to go to the bathroom. And she asked if I was faking it.

They transferred me to Fairmont in a room with five or six other people, but I didn't know at first; I was still out of it. My mother said she couldn't understand why they didn't clean all the glass, dirt, and weeds out of my hair. So days after I woke up she had me put into a wheelchair and rolled me to the sink in my hospital room to wash my hair. As she prepared me for the shampoo, some black nurses started hanging around and calling other nurses they knew to come over, discussing whether my hair was going to puff up and get nappy when my mother wet it. My mother yelled out, "Can I please have some privacy!"

As my brain started to wake up, I realized they had me in a bed with bars on each side. My consciousness started coming back to me a little at a time. I knew when I needed to go to the bathroom. One day I woke up and wanted a bath. Little bits of my personality came drifting back. My friend Eduard said I put my hands up in front of my face and looked at them. He wondered what I was doing and then realized that I wanted my rings. He went to the junk jewelry department at Bay Fair Mall and bought me some costume jewelry—he brought me back two big fake rings.

It took a long time for me to come to myself. But I still wasn't fully there yet. I wasn't able to grasp all of what I was being told, but what I did understand wasn't good news at all. I had a broken neck, broken ribs, a bruised heart, a cracked-open skull, a crushed pelvic bone, two sprained ankles, and a bunch of scars. One of the other things that happened that I didn't know about at the time, was that I'd lost a lot of blood. At first, my family didn't want me to receive any transfusions. This was during the height of the AIDS epidemic, and people were frightened that donated blood might be contaminated. The doctors were finally able to convince them that they would be able to supply me with blood that wasn't tainted. I was told that the doctors had not expected me to wake up at all and that if I did, they'd expected I would be paralyzed and a vegetable.

My friend Eduard told me that during those days after the accident, he could see that I wasn't remembering my relatives. He said that I would frown at my mom as if I couldn't quite place her. One day when she was speaking to me, she said, "Can you call me Mom?"

I looked at her and said, "Oh, so that's what you want to be called?"

I didn't say it to be cruel; I honestly couldn't remember her. I didn't understand why all these people were coming to see me when I didn't know them from any other strangers.

As hard as my recovery was, the emotional damage was devastating as well. My body was riddled with pain. Some days were hard and other days were worse. As my body began to slowly heal, I was faced with the question: why did this happen to me, and where was God?

Before the accident, I had been on the fence with my faith. I believed in God but was upset with Him because of situations in my life that I'd gone through. But I believed in following His ways. When I woke up from this coma, I wrote: "I thank God to be alive. He promised me to life all the nights I cried. I say it's better to live and let live than to be two days from death, then die. Please God, be always by my side." But I wasn't happy with Him.

As a kid, I got beat up in school all the time, ganged up on by kids who were jealous. When I was in seventh grade, I was dealing with a girl named Verilyn. I thought we were friends. We had been talking to each other for a few weeks and were walking home one day. When we got to my house, I was about to go inside, and she asked if she could use my bathroom. My father was outside, getting ready to leave, and he told her, "You're not far from your house; please go home and use your own bathroom." A few days later she asked to use my comb. I told her my mother didn't like me doing that because kids pass lice to each other that way.

Next thing I know, Verilyn was no longer talking to me. But she had plenty of nasty things to say to other kids about me. I was supposedly stuck up. She started having other kids in school do things to me.

Once they put gum on my chair and watched me sit down in it and laughed. I heard one of the girls say, "We should put it on the back of her chair so she'll get it in her hair." In my home economics class, another girl came up to me and said, "What would you do if somebody cut your face up and cut all your hair off?" What was she expecting me to say? How did she expect me to feel? This question took my joy and made me feel sad, confused, and scared. I wondered why I was going through all this. After that day I started wearing my hair up in a bun because I never knew if someone sitting behind me in class might try to cut my hair off.

Every day as my mother would drive me to school, the closer I got, the sicker I'd become. My forehead and hands would sweat, my hands would have the feeling of pins and needles, and my stomach would get gassy and upset so that my mother would have to pull the car over so I could throw up. This is no exaggeration. I wouldn't even eat breakfast in the morning because I knew I would throw it up. "Why am I going to school?" I would ask myself. To be tortured and abused? For nothing. It was so awful to go to school and always have to worry about my physical safety, never knowing what was going to happen from day to day.

Another one of the people Verilyn got to bully me was a girl named Penny. She was an eleventh or twelfth grader, too old to be messing around with us seventh- and eighth-grade kids. I didn't even know her. Penny physically attacked me on the bus one day just because Verilyn asked her to do it.

That same year, my cousin was in a boating accident. He had his two sons with him, both of whom died. The kids from our school came to the service because many of them were the boy's classmates. At the end of the service, Penny stood on the steps in front of the church. She laughed and said, "I'm glad he's dead." My family was absolutely shocked. My sister asked why anyone would say such a thing. My father went as far as to get a restraining order against Penny after that.

We didn't need it for long. Coincidentally, Penny got sick with an allergy of some sort, her lungs filled up with fluid, and she suffocated. Rumor has it she died four days after my cousin's funeral.

After Penny died, no one from Verilyn's clique bothered me again.

Later, when I went to Hayward High, I was sitting one day in my English class when a girl grabbed my right arm at the wrist and put the palm of my hand next to her palm and asked, "I don't understand why your hand is more white than mine and I'm white!" I snatched my hand back, wondering why anyone would ask such a petty question. So I told her, "You need to go home and talk to your mother about it."

On my way to my next class, a group of girls came up behind me, swinging their legs up as if about to kick me. I heard one of them laugh and say, "Get her! Kick her right in the middle of her butt!" I turned around and looked at the two black girls behind me and they just smiled at me. I didn't even know these two girls, but yet they wanted to hurt me. This is what the sin of jealousy makes you do.

One day, a girl named Bridget walked up to me while I was sitting outside and threw a whole carton of milk on me. I asked her why she would do such a thing, and she stood there and laughed. I went to tell an adult what happened to me, and she just said, "I don't believe you. I don't see any milk on you." I said my jacket had absorbed it and asked her to feel my jacket. Nothing was done about it.

I dealt with a lot of racism from other students. That's why they beat me up. I was beat up by black kids all the time. I was waiting outside the portable of my next class in junior high when a classmate named Morsche walked up behind me, tapped me on my shoulder, and said, "You think dark-skinned black people are ugly." I told her not to put words in my mouth, that I had never said that. My mom used to transfer me from school to school, hoping to find somewhere I wouldn't get abused. But it didn't help. I still got beat up at school.

Wow! The day of graduation finally came. I was walking the stage at Skyline High. I was getting my Diploma. I felt a sense of relief off of my shoulders. When my name was called to proceed to the stage to get my diploma, tears fell from my eyes as I walked to the stage. I accepted my diploma from the principal and walked back to my seat on cloud nine, believing all this mess I'd been through, through the years at all the schools I'd attended, was over.

I sat down at my seat outside on this warm, blue, sunny day, and the principal and his staff asked all the students to stand up and move our tassels to the other side of our hats to signify our graduation and move on to the next stage of our life. Then the announcer said, "You are now all graduates; throw your hats up in the air!" Well, before I could move my tassel, one of those nasty girls stole it off my hat before I could throw it up in the air. At graduation my joy was stolen once again. Why are people so petty and cruel?

After that, going to lunch one day with my friend Eduard, he looked over at me and said, "What brings such a big smile?" I looked at him and said, "I have finally graduated, and all the nasty things those girls did to me are over."

Eduard replied, "Oh, no, baby; it now just becomes more sophisticated."

I was even chased out of the BayFair Mall by strangers that swung bats and pipes at me. Eduard ran me out of the mall for my safety. The mall security saw the excitement and rushed over to help.

People can ask me all day what race I am or tell me what they think I am. And I will never answer them. I have never understood why people feel the need to distinguish people and put them into boxes based on race, how they look, or the things people have. I am not going to be put into categories, whether regarding gender or race, skin color, or what I have in life. To me, there is only one thing that matters, and that's God. We are all flesh, and when we die, we return to ashes, and all ashes are the same.

• • • •

When I was released from ICU at Highland Hospital in Oakland, CA, I was transferred to rehab at Fairmont Hospital in San Leandro, CA, to continue my journey in healing. A bag of my personal belongings was given to my dear friend Eduard for safekeeping until I was ready to go home.

Months later when I returned home, I was given this bag of things that I couldn't understand, because I had no memory of what had happened. It was like somebody stole my life! It all looked so odd. My clothes were ripped, and blood was on everything. Eduard explained that all my clothes had been cut off of me while I lay there on the street after the accident.

Eduard then told me his friend had an Omega necklace in his Oakland store that looked like one I was wearing at the time of the accident, and it was scraped up. I went to look at it and, yes, it was mine. How could this be? How could my cousin take my things off my broken and potentially dead body and pawned them to get money as I lay there in the streets? That's cold! I broke down and cried. That's family for you. My friend Eduard contacted his friend, and the necklace was returned to me.

I didn't remember the accident at all nor did I know who I was. The doctor said that was normal because of the trauma to my head. Then one night, as I lay in bed trying to fall asleep, I was shown something like a video in my mind of what had happened to me in that accident. I thought to myself "now I know". I saw it image by image in slow motion of my body bouncing around like a basketball game. Now the horror of the image was in my mind. All I could do was rewind and replay over and over again. I started to have negative thoughts.

Then some statements started to pop into my head. "Look what happened to you. Look at what God allowed to be done to you. He doesn't care about you!" All the little things from my life—the slips and falls—as well as all the other ugly things that had happened to me combined into this new disappointment. The stupid things which shouldn't have happened to me in the first place. Everything came to a head with this accident, it was like icing on a cake.

Days turned into weeks, weeks into months, and months into years. My mind and body needed healing before I could grapple with the pain in my soul. I was hurt both inside and out. I didn't know what to do; I was broken. Thoughts of death did occur. But when healing happened, it came in the most unexpected and beautiful way.

One day, I was put in a wheelchair and wheeled out to the deck outside a great room with tables and a television in the corner. It was a bright, warm, sunny day outside. Many people were there, all smiling at me. "Tamiko, your family is so happy to see you," the nurse told me. I just stared at them. I had no idea who they were. How could these people be my family? I was convinced the nurse had to be wrong. It's just the weirdest thing when you look at people and haven't got the slightest idea who they are. All I kept thinking, as I was still suffering from amnesia as well as the aftereffects of the coma, was, *Who are these people?*

There were instructions in my chart that I wasn't supposed to be moved without the use of a wheelchair because of my crushed pelvis from the accident. The bars were also supposed to be kept up whenever I was in bed. One night a nurse came to my room to help me go to the bathroom, but she didn't read my chart. She didn't speak English. I don't know if she thought I could walk and refused to cooperate, or why she didn't realize something was wrong. She pulled me up from the bed and tried to make me walk. Still out of it, I tried but kept falling down. The nurse kept trying to pull me down the hallway to the bathroom. Another nurse saw what she was doing and came running over with a wheelchair. Screaming repeatedly at the other nurse to leave me alone, she explained, "She's not supposed to walk." The nurse who rescued me put me in the wheelchair herself while the other nurse stood there staring, looking as dumb as could be.

I presume I eventually made it to the bathroom because the next thing I recall was being back in my bed again. It bothers me when I hear about people getting hurt over things like this. Some people simply don't care about what they are doing wrong. People are quick to judge and hurt others, but they wouldn't want to be treated that way themselves. I was only ninety pounds with scars. She knew I couldn't walk.

Another nurse who worked in the Fairmont Hospital stole from me. She knew I was not in my right mind; have these people no self-respect nor integrity? When something is wrong, it's wrong. There is no excuse for taking advantage of helpless people. Stop and look at your reactions before you act upon them. Think before you speak.

The nurse assigned to me was told that I could not have a bath. I pressed for a bath to the point where the head nurse finally allowed it, but I had to be watched and was allowed very little water in the tub. This was part of the protocol for patients when taking baths.

As I got ready to take my bath, Nurse Naomi told me I had to take off my rings and leave them in the drawer. I watched her open the drawer and put the rings inside. "You can get them back when you're out of the tub," she told me.

Naomi helped me take off my clothes and get into the tub. She put very little water in the tub and stood leaning up against the wall, watching me in the tub. "I will be right back," she said, and left me in the tub by myself.

Naomi knew I was not supposed to be left in that bathtub alone at all! After a few minutes, she came back. "It's time for you to get out of the tub now." Naomi dressed me, put me back in the wheelchair, and rolled me back to my hospital room. When I looked in the drawer where Naomi had put my rings, they were gone. I told the head nurse that Naomi told me to take off my rings and when I came back from my bath, they were gone. She said she would handle it but didn't comment any further. Shortly after that, I had a new nurse. When I asked about Naomi, one of the other nurses said she had been sent to a different part of the hospital to work on another floor.

One of the many things I will always appreciate about Dr. Kaswani, even though I was still having problems remembering things and communicating properly, when I complained about what was going on with me, he actually listened. I didn't know it at that point, but big changes were about to happen because he was concerned about the care I was receiving.

The next time I saw Naomi was months later after I was released from the hospital. I was with my mother and sister in Macy's. She yelled at me, saying I had gotten her in trouble with her job. Didn't she know I was still mentally disabled? I couldn't handle any kind of conflict. I couldn't understand at the time what she was telling me.

• • • •

Back to my recovery, as I became increasingly alert, I began to act a little more like myself. There was a girl two beds down from me in the hospital room; only a set of drapes separated us. One night, I woke up and heard a snorting sound. The girl lay in her bed with the safety rails up and tubes attached to different parts of her body. She was out, maybe in a coma or something. I couldn't sleep because that sound irritated me. I was hypersensitive to it. I told Dr. Kaswani and the nurse that I wanted my own room. They said I couldn't get one, so I said, "You'd better find a room for me."

Nurses used to come in and out at all times of the day and night. My friends would bring me magazines to keep me up on the latest fashions. It was a small thing, but any diversion helped break up the daily monotony.

One day, a male orderly put me on a gurney to take me to two appointments I had in the hospital. While he pushed me, he sang, "Are You Down with the OPP? Yeah, You Know Me." (For those who don't know, opp means other people's privates.)

When I arrived at the doctor's appointment, the doctor looked inside my ear. Then he took a wire and scratched around inside my ear. "Do not move; it will damage your eardrum." He used the wire to remove blood and wax from the accident. I lay there scared and trembling, stiff as a board on the table, not knowing nor understanding what he was doing. I felt pricks of pain and pressure listening to this sound of horror inside my head. I found out later from Kaiser Hospital that he should have used a peroxide and water lavage flush to get it out instead of an instrument. This doctor had an orthotic shoe on his right foot with a thick sole that looked like it was six inches, and his other shoe was normal. He had a limp. I remembered that.

At my next appointment, a doctor had me lie down on my stomach on the gurney with my arms hanging off from the elbows down. While he was looking at my back, for some reason, he kept rubbing his penis on my elbow. When you're suffering from trauma, you either remember things vividly or they quickly fade.

About two weeks later, I finally moved into a single room, right next to the bathroom. I loved it, loved it, loved it. I was so happy to have a little privacy. I was at Fairmont for a little over two months, but having my own space made it much more bearable.

Dr. Kaswani met with my family to update them on my status. I was not allowed in this meeting. He was going to allow me to be released early because I wanted to get out of Fairmont due to the poor treatment and abuse I'd experienced. My body had not fully healed yet, and he let them know that I shouldn't be allowed to walk, nor was I to be left alone unsupervised. According to the doctor, people with head injuries like mine often became depressed because of problems with their memory. They often try to kill themselves. I couldn't be allowed into the kitchen or bathroom by myself, or be allowed to handle sharp objects at any time. My sister took two months off of work to help me.

When the day came for me to leave rehab at Fairmont, I was so happy. It had been a long haul, and I was looking forward to going home. No one would take my things or talk to me cruelly anymore. I wouldn't have to make a federal case just to take a bath. I would have food and wouldn't have to keep asking for my meals anymore.

While waiting in my hospital room, my sister came in to let me know she was signing papers for my discharge and would be right back. A few minutes later a nurse came in and handed me a pair of crutches. She walked away without speaking to me. I used the crutches to come out of the room. A maintenance man was mopping the floor just outside my door.

The front desk was to the right of my room. When I stepped onto the wet floor, I slipped and fell hard onto my butt. "I'm so sorry!" the maintenance man apologized emphatically. "I didn't know anyone was in that room!" My sister ran over to pick me up, but none of the nurses at the front desk moved or even said a word to me. They just stared at me.

The head nurse came with a wheelchair. "Don't you ever come back here."

I spoke to Dr. Kaswani after I was out of the hospital, and he told me that no one had notified him of the fall. "If only I'd known, I could have reset you," he said. "They didn't tell me. I'm so sorry. I can't do anything now; it is too late." As it was, I'd have to work with the injuries I'd sustained. My spine and hips are completely twisted like a candy cane. With that bad news and the excruciating pain, I cried and thought to myself "what am I going to do?". I started drinking and popping pills for relief. My friend Eduard found a hospital named – The Spine Center- in Daly City California. He took me there and I spoke to the Doctor asking him to re-break the bones to fix my body so that the pain would stop. The diagnosis was that he could do nothing for me. So my suffering and depression continued. I learned about chiropractors, so I now go to them for therapy and to keep from getting migraines.

I don't want to wear an orthopedic boot; I'm into fashion!

I tried to sue Fairmont for medical misconduct. By law, whenever you are being discharged you are supposed to be wheeled out of the hospital in a wheelchair. If I hadn't been discharged on crutches, I wouldn't have had the fall in the first place.

I kept hearing this one phrase from friends and family over and over again. "After the way they treated you, those people owe you a house." I spoke to the head of the Fairmont Hospital, Michael Smart, and tried to the best of my ability to explain to him the situation of the fall. I still had stuttering issues and my speech pattern was terribly affected by the trauma to the head. I would have the sentences right in my mind, but would come out confused. Michael Smart recognized this, so he told me to send him a letter about what happened to me during my stay. What none of these people seemed to realize and grasp was that I was still confused and couldn't fully understand what I was being told. Since people kept talking about houses, I mailed this man a picture of a house. I wasn't in my right mind.

When I called the hospital to speak to him again, he told his secretary to tell me never to call him again.

A few years passed and I called Fairmont Hospital again, asking for help. This time it was Mr. Lasiter. I was calling him since he was the newly appointed CEO. I explained what happened to me and I asked them to pay for my medical costs due to the slip and fall in their hospital. He told me that he did not care and the hospital would give me nothing. How can these people, these CEO's of a hospital, whose job it is to help those that are injured, who have the medical records of my accident, know what happened to me and know I was hurt at their facility, just continue to ignore me and have absolutely no compassion for people. No attorney wanted this slip and fall case because they felt there wasn't enough reward "money" for them. That fall caused me a magnitude of problems, and not once did they think of the medical care I needed. So I was left to physically heal wrong and suffer. Pro per was the only way I could move forward.

When the case went to court, Judge Winifred Weismith said I had no cause. I wanted to know how a statute could apply to me when I hadn't been well enough to walk for so long or was allowed to leave the house because of my mental state, much less appear in court. When I told him that I was mentally disabled, he said I needed to show proof. I got copies of medical reports from Fairmont Hospital showing Dr. Kaswani confirming that I was not mentally stable.

None of my efforts did me any good. Fairmont ended up getting away without having to pay a single cent for their negligence, the pain and suffering they caused, and all of the rehabilitation I needed and still need as a result of my poor treatment.

This is just another example of how people feel it's fine to do anything to others, yet they don't want to be treated that way themselves. People lack the integrity to stand up and admit to their mistakes, taking responsibility for the things they do and the way they act.

I was upset with God. I felt like He had failed me yet again.

Chapter 6

How Could You?

Suzette is my first cousin; her mother is my mom's sister. She and her family used to come up to the hospital and visit me all the time until my little sister spoke with the staff and asked only to let immediate family in to see me. By the time I was released, it had been months since I had seen Suzette.

After I was released from Fairmont, I stole my car from Eduard's house and would drive to places I remembered. One of the places I would drive to was Suzette's house in Oakland.

One day my sister was with me and said, "We're gonna start making you look like a person again. We'll do your hair and put you in some clothes. Let's look in your closet." After trying on some clothes, she said, "Girl, you look lost in those pants." I had to agree with her. I had lost so much weight that everything just hung on me.

My sister washed and set my hair, put me in some clothes, applied a bit of makeup, and I was on my way driving to my cousin Suzette's house. Suzette was getting married and had asked me to be a bridesmaid in her wedding; I accepted. We looked at a lot of dresses that she found in the bridal magazines. I had been at her house for a while so I told Suzy I was a little tired and ready to go home. Don't forget I had recently been released from the hospital from the coma.

Suzy stopped me as I was walking to the front door. "Don't go just yet; I want you to see a scene in the movie *Pure Luck*." I said okay and sat back down on the couch. Suzette sat down in front of the television on her knees. I sat on the left-hand side of the couch, and her sister sat on a stool behind me. The front door was to the left of us.

The doorbell rang and it was Suzette's fiancé. He came in and she introduced us. He sat down on the couch to the right of me. I became uncomfortable because he kept staring at me. I turned and looked directly at him to see what he was staring at, and then I looked down. That is when I saw a lump in his pants.

Since I had just gotten out of the hospital, I was not in my right mind yet. Sometimes it would take time for my mind to interpret what the eyes were seeing, and I couldn't believe what I was seeing. It was like a train wreck. I didn't want to look, but I kept looking. He was having a hard-on while staring at me!

Suzette's sister saw this and walked up to me. "You need to leave and go home to your own man," she snapped.

I was confused. "I don't have a man," I said. "What are you talking about?"

I looked at Suzette, wondering if she would tell her sister to stop this foolishness. "She's right," Suzette said. "You need to leave right now."

After that day, Suzette stopped talking to me. She didn't want me in her wedding. Within no time she started telling lies about me to the family. My aunt Aloma went up to Granny's house and told her and my other aunt Tamara that I had tried to steal Suzette's man. Luckily my auntie Tamara and granny knew better, put her in her place, and told her, "Miki wouldn't do a thing like that." My sister said the whole story was BS, too.

After that, we stopped dealing with Suzette. She ended up marrying that guy. Aloma later revealed to me that Suzette was having serious problems in her marriage. She should have understood that him checking me out while in her house was a sign that her man wasn't going to be faithful.

Years later, I saw her again in a mall. She had the nerve to say hello to my sister, mother, and me as if nothing had happened. I lost it on her. I was ready to put my foot in her you-know-what! "How can you come over here and smile in my face after what you accused me of?" I demanded. "I wasn't going to touch your man! I don't believe in that. He obviously didn't even want you."

She started crying and told me it wasn't like that. I told her I didn't want to hear it or see her ever again, and she had no right to talk to anybody in my family. She knew very well I hadn't made a pass at her man. She just wanted to protect her relationship. Her fiancé was on a farm league baseball team, which is a group of players practicing for the major leagues. He had given her a two-karat diamond ring. This is the ugliness of things in the world. Getting that money from her man was more important than being kind to me. It didn't matter that she probably knew he was a dog; she wasn't going to let that stand in the way of her getting the material things she wanted in life.

Once again, I was wrongfully accused, this time by my first cousin. I was beginning to wonder when it was going to end. When were people going to stop singling me out for things I didn't do or wasn't responsible for? I have more integrity than to try to steal anyone's man. How could my family members, who knew me better than anyone else, doubt me? After I had been so sick, having almost lost my life and dealt with so many injuries, the last thing on my mind was chasing anybody's man. But once again I was bitter and hurt because God hadn't stopped people from harming me.

Chapter 7

No Apology

I was at lunch with Eduard one day when a woman approached me. She saw that I was having trouble moving, and she gave me the name of a chiropractor who had done her wonders. She told me that she had sports-related injuries over the years and she thought this doctor, Dr. Leonard, might be able to do wonders for me.

She gave me the doctor's card. I called the office the next day and was able to make an appointment.

I had several visits with Dr. Leonard. About a month into our sessions, she told me that she was going to go on a vacation. She wanted me to know that I would be seen by someone else on my following doctor's visit.

The substitute doctor was a man by the name of Mikleboost. When I laid down on the table, he pulled my pants down and exposed my naked bottom.

"What are you doing?" I cried. I pulled my pants back up. He just stood there and looked at me like I had some nerve, and then he walked out. I got out of that office as fast as I could. How could he think that he would get away with that?

When Dr. Leonard came back, I told her what happened. Her eyes got as wide as saucers, but she didn't say anything.

It wasn't until I told Eduard about what happened that I found out the doctor who had touched me was her husband. I would have sued, but Dr. Leonard had been so good to me. She put in a lot of work to get me back on the road to being rehabilitated. So since she had been there for me, I decided not to sue. I didn't want to destroy her career by going after him.

Here's What's Going to Happen
I Don't Care
What Race or Religion You Are
You Have No Reverential Fear
For The Things You Do in Life

Jesus Didn't Die
For Us to Have a Title

He Gave Us Rules
To Protect Us
From Our Own Slaughter

When It Comes Right Down to It
You Are Only Sorry
Before Your Day of Death

Thinking You Can Do Your Daily Evil
And Be Forgiven the Next Day
Well, That's Not How It Works

You Were Given a Conscience
To Know Right from Wrong
Why Can't You Understand
You Can't Rewrite the Bible

No One Is Walking This Earth
Without Knowing Our Father
He Tells You Time and Time Again
You Will Reap What You Sow

Humans Have Gone Too Far
And Thinking Was Not Involved

People Are So Ugly
Because of a Race, Job Title, Sex, or Religion
With Their Lying, Cheating, and Stealing

Believing in Their Opinions
That Gives Them the Right to Judge

This Flesh
Has This Attitude

That Thinks
It's Holier Than Thou

It Runs Amuck
Mocking His Word

Time
Time Is Running Short
You Can Listen to Me or Not

The Horns Will Blow
If You're Not Ready
You Will Be Left Here
To Rot

There Is
No Second Chance
This Time

Your Ignorance
Of Free Will Is Misleading
Because a Servant
Is Not Greater Than His Master

Almighty
Is the One That Will Judge You
There Is
Only One God
As You Are on Your Knees
Bowing Down to Him

I Have Been Around the Block
So Many Times
I Understand Just What's Going On

It's Senseless to Think
We Can Fix This
The Greed and Selfishness
Is Beyond Belief

I Don't Know
How to Explain It
To Change It
To Help the World
Become a Better Place
I Just Sit, Listen, and Watch
As My Brain
Records These Images of Chaos

The Abruptions
People Encounter
From One Another

Carry That Nastiness
To Another Day
To Give
To Another Person

The Power of the Flesh
Is Intoxicating
It's Scandalous

What It Sees
It Will Take
In the Decisions
That It Makes

You Want Control
Over Something That's Not Yours
Living with What You Wanted
And Thought You Deserved

Hahaha Did You Ever Get It?

It's Sad to Say
The Sins
We Keep Reliving

The Suffering
The Sickness
Runs So Deep

How Do You
Hold Your Head Up
From Your Lies
And Deceit?

Before You Claim What You Did

And Not Beg for Forgiveness
It's Just Disgusting
As We Walk Over Everybody
Every Day
With Another Form of Slavery

We Gave Our Authority
To the Devil

It Just Took
That Once

He Took Our
Better Interest
And Threw Our
Pearls to the Hogs

All We Had to Do
Was Follow and Abide
By One Golden Rule

You Bit That Apple
We Failed
And We Still
Don't Get It

To This Day
Where We Stand
Still after This
Dissatisfaction

Our Father Is There
When You Need Him
From Our Father's
True Love of Commitment

He Has a New Plan
For Restoration

Which Brings Us
To My Secret

Of What
I Was Told to Tell

It Doesn't Matter
If You Want to Listen

Or Not

You Will Still Hear
From Word of Mouth

Our Father Works
Through People

I Was Chosen
Before I Was Born

I Am
The Chosen One
To Spread His Word

Not to Fix This World
But to Prepare You
For What Is to Come

Chapter 8

I Wish It Would Stop

While I was in college, I held down a couple of part-time jobs. I enjoyed keeping busy, and it also helped me afford one of my favorite pursuits—shopping. I applied for a job at Apple One, hoping to pick up a part-time gig that would come in handy.

I spoke with a recruiter named Amber. She told me about a job that she said no one wanted. The pay per hour was reasonable, and the duties were simple: answering the phone, typing, filing, and greeting anyone who came in—a basic receptionist job. The woman who usually worked there was on a pregnancy leave and would be back in about two months. Since it was a healthcare company, I let her know that I had worked with disabled adults in the past. I told her that sounded perfect, and she submitted my resume for it. Next thing I knew, I was going in on a Monday to start work.

I realized pretty quickly that this was one of those jobs where I would have to figure things out for myself. I was given a list of extensions in the office so I would know where to direct the calls to various workers, but I wasn't trained on their phone system. A basket of paperwork needed filing, and I organized it alphabetically so I could file it later.

The manager, Mrs. Turnbull, took me around the office and introduced me to the staff. This company was a home health agency that sent out nurses to the homes of people who were ill. Many of their patients were either elderly, disabled, or people recently released from the hospital who required care. I tried to remember everyone's names, but a few of them had offices in the back and I never really saw them after that first introduction.

That afternoon, I got a call from an impatient woman. I asked her who she needed to talk to. She replied with a torrent of cuss words I'm not even comfortable repeating. She cussed me out, called me a racial slur, and tied it up with a bunch of other nonsense. I put her on hold.

I went to the back where the two managers, Ms. Turnbull and Bob, were talking with other employees. It sounded more like a casual conversation than a meeting. I knocked on the door and politely asked if someone could take this call, as this woman had already called me every name and had even gotten racial about it.

"Who is it?" Mrs. Turnbull asked.

"I haven't been able to get the woman's name. All she's done is yell and cuss me out. Can you take her call? Can someone tell her to stop talking to me like that? It's very unprofessional."

Mrs. Turnbull and Bob looked at each other and laughed. "Oh yes, I know who that is. She works for us. She's from the main office. She has bipolar disorder and that's just the way she talks. I'll take that call. Go ahead and transfer her."

I went back to my desk and tried to shake off the whole incident. I hoped that I wouldn't have to deal with this crazy person again, but the odds weren't good since she was one of their employees.

Later on that day, when I was filing, Mrs. Turnbull came over to my desk. She didn't say anything, but I felt her staring at me. I wore a big ring that day a friend had given me, along with my wedding ring. The way she looked at my jewelry gave me an uncomfortable feeling. I could tell she didn't like what she saw. Some people think they can hide their jealousy when they really can't.

The next morning went fairly smooth—there were no calls from the dreaded employee with the foul mouth. What was weird was that everyone came that day dressed up, hair done. The women even tried to dress like me. It was the oddest thing I had ever seen. By midmorning one of the staff members came around and started rifling through the sorter on my desk that held the papers to be filed.

"I can't find anything," she complained. "You know these are not how I like my papers filed."

"Excuse me," I said. "Who are you again?"

She fussed with me, but I told her that I was filing the paperwork the way Mrs. Turnbull had told me to; maybe she should speak with my supervisor if she had questions about it. She stormed off, cussing under her breath.

By lunchtime I was feeling hot and uncomfortable. I decided to go home, shower, and change during my lunch break. I barely had enough time, but I rushed through afternoon traffic and made it back to my desk with a few minutes to spare. I hadn't been there long when Carmen came up to my desk. She was one of the managers, and for the most part, always seemed to be on the phone or chatting with Ms. Turnbull.

Carmen approached me with a smile, and I smiled back. I was sure that she was going to ask me to do something for her, or maybe ask me what happened with the other person who had complained about the filing earlier.

"Hey Tamiko, I just have to know. We were in the back talking about it and I would like to know. Which one is white and which one is the Negro in your parents?"

"What?" I asked. I couldn't believe she had even approached me like that!

"This is a place of business. I don't talk about things like that."

As I walked back to my desk, she seemed disappointed. The phone rang and I was happy for the distraction. I picked up the call and she walked away.

Toward the end of the day Bob came up to my desk. "Well, we know all the cars in the parking lot, and yours wasn't there. So we walked around the block and found yours. You must own Apple One, and you're just working here because you're bored."

I told him, "This is a place of business, and my personal life has nothing to do with you."

I was happy to call it a day. I got a call from Apple One after I got home. They said the assignment had been ended. When I asked why, they told me that the employer had told them I was unable to complete simple tasks like filing, alphabetizing, and that I wasn't able to read. I was so mad. When I spoke to Amber, I told her they knew that wasn't true; I was in college and they had all my credentials before they even hired me. They knew that job was well below my capabilities. So how was it that all of a sudden they didn't believe me?

Amber told me that I needed to go someplace else and look for work elsewhere. Apple One never called me for work ever again.

But jealousy never works for people. I called Home Care Options a month later because I needed to confirm their names for a complaint I was going to file with the EEOC over the way I had been treated. The receptionist told me that none of the previous managers were there anymore. Someone had bought out the company and all of them had been let go. After that I decided it was best to just let it go.

Look At This World
We Live In

Wait a Minute
You Know
You're Living in It

It Feels Like were in the Ice Age
Humans Are Cold . . . Hearted
Living in Ways
That Is Not Lord Supported

It Doesn't Matter
Where You're From
It's in Your City, State, Zip Code Maybe
Even Your Own Hometown
This Evil Makes You Frown

Nobody Wants to Be Responsible
For Their Inappropriate, Cruel, or Illegal Ways

You Did It, Claim It
You Should Know
Your Gonna Pay for It

It's Senseless to Believe
You Think You're Not Wrong
For These
Inexcusable Things

The Lord Is Disappointed
That His Children Fail Him

His Task
We're Left with Examples
We Try to Rewrite
'Cause We Don't Want to Believe
Nor Do Them

These Rules
Were for Your Protection
No Sex before Marriage
No Lies, No Cheating, Nor Stealing
It Goes On
And On
It's Deep
But You Still
Don't Want to Believe

This Disrespect
We Have for One Another
And the Self-Respect
That Costs About a Dollar

The Lord Cries with Sorrow
Because You Keep
Coming Up with Excuses
Believing He's Going to Forgive

And Then You
Do It Again Tomorrow

You Know
You Reap What You Sow

But People Such As Yourself
Today
Want to Be Deaf, Dumb, and Blind

To Live the Life
They Chose
For Their Own
Insidious Satisfaction
That's Out of Control

Chapter 9

Almost Famous

When I was young, my mother, sister, and I would gather downstairs and watch old movies on the American Movie Channel. One of our favorites was the movie called *Sparkle*. This was the original *Sparkle* that starred Lonette McKee in the title role. The story is about a man attracted to a woman that he sees in a photo. He treats her like a queen and is a constant gentleman to her, and soon they become an item. That is where the story shifts. Although he attests his love for her, he becomes jealous of her talent, beauty, and the amount of attention she gets. He then begins the process of breaking her down by abusing her physically, emotionally, and spiritually. He gets her hooked on drugs, and eventually she spirals out of control until the point that she loses everything she had and everything she was.

Although this movie is fiction, there is a lot of truth behind it. There are men who do these types of things to women out of jealousy. Even as a child, I could not understand how a man could be jealous of a woman and vice versa. You are different sexes, have different things to offer society, differing thoughts, opinions, and emotions. When you break it down even to the basics of evolution, they have different roles in creating life. That is why God created woman and man. We are different from each other, yet when combined, we are one in harmony.

Fast forward to 1996. I used to go clubbing with one of my cousins. We had differing tastes in music; however, we had an agreement that she would go to the shows I liked and in return I would go to those she liked. One night we ended up at Kimble's East in Emeryville. I was wearing one of my favorite pieces, a blue leather outfit.

While I was in the ladies' room, a woman named Renee came up and introduced herself to me. I am an open person and embrace people with open arms, even strangers. She invited me to go back to her table to watch the show and have some drinks.

A man at the club that night, Larry Blackman, had spoken to Renee and let her know he was interested in meeting me. I told Renee that I didn't know who he was and asked why he couldn't come over and speak to me himself.

Larry sent a bottle of wine over to the table. Though his gesture was nice, I was not going to drink it. One thing I always do when I go out is bring my own bottle of water with me in my bag. I always want to be in control when out in crowds, especially when I'm driving. My grandmother had told me a long time ago, "Miki, when you get old enough to go out, whenever you order a drink, never turn your back on that drink. If you do, consider that drink gone because somebody may have put something in your drink in the hopes of getting you high and taking advantage of you."

Shortly after that, Larry came over and introduced himself to me. He put out his arm and escorted me to another table where we could talk without all the crowd noise. He was nice and such a gentleman; we had a good time. At the end of the night we exchanged phone numbers. It was a wonderful friendship at first, or so I thought. We spent a lot of late nights laughing over the phone, talking about food, commercials, movies, books we had read, and everyday life. Then we started going places together, to dinners and shows. Larry then invited me to fly out to New York with him to see what he did. I said yes, and the next thing I knew we were flying to New York.

While in New York I met Larry's assistant, Kat. I spent more time with Kat than I did with Larry to the point that I joked with her that it felt like I was dating her. She got a kick out of that and agreed. I was having a lot of fun, going to parties, meeting new people, and having people tell me that if I was interested in getting into the music industry, to give them a call. They would hand me their business card and I would put them in my clutch. I was told that these were private and serious parties.

Larry was all about appearances and always had to be the center of attention. He apparently did not care for the attention I got at these parties because when we would get back to the hotel, he would grab my clutch and pull all the business cards out. He told me, "I need to know who my friends are." I felt disbelief.

We sat at a table for a while and talked, laughing a little. Then from nowhere he told me I was being sneaky, only using the phone when he was not around. I told Larry I had nothing to hide. I had called my mother, my grandmother, and Eduard to let them know I'd arrived safely in New York.

"Give me the phone bill and I will pay for all three calls that I made,"

"Why is this a problem? My family wanted to make sure I was okay. You were in meetings and I was left in my room." He blew smoke in my face, not once but twice. I simply looked at him and told him,

"Stop that; don't blow smoke in my face!" I didn't know what point he was trying to get across, but it angered me, so I told him I was going to retire for the night. I stood up and left the room.

The next day we were to fly back to California. He had made this trip ugly for me by giving me nothing but attitude, and it made me feel uncomfortable. We stopped by a house full of people before we left for the airport; one of them was his mother. He introduced us, but she did not have much to say to me. We then flew back to California, where I returned to my apartment and crashed.

A few days passed. My phone was silent until late one night when Larry called to tell me jokes, and the good times started again. A little more time passed, and Larry called to see if I wanted to join him for another trip. I said, "Sure. Where are we going?" Twenty three hours later we arrived in Japan.

By the time we got to the hotel there, I was exhausted. I asked Larry to give me a few minutes to get myself together. He completely understood and told me he would come back later to check on me. I soon fell asleep. Larry later told me that he had come back to check on me and since I was sound asleep, he pulled the blankets over me and left for his show. I was asleep for hours, and before I knew it we were packing up to head back to the States. I wondered how Larry did this—get up, get ready, and go at the drop of a dime.

A few days later, one of Larry's flunkies showed up at my apartment door. I don't know if Larry sent him to check on me or to make sure there wasn't someone else at my place; either way all I do know is that I did not care for it one bit. I definitely let him know to never come to my apartment again, and Larry got an earful from me later that night. Larry mentioned he would be in my neck of the woods the next day and wanted to stop by. I later mentioned to Eduard that Larry would be stopping by the next day.

The next day, within twenty minutes of arriving home from work, Larry knocked at my door. I invited him in, and he took a seat on a chair in my bedroom as I cleaned up. No sooner had he sat down than he immediately jumped up and ran out of my apartment like a bat out of hell with an attitude, yelling and screaming at me the whole time. I asked him to slow down and explain why he was yelling at me. He said I was screwing another man in my bedroom. I told him I wasn't and asked why he was saying that.

He continued to yell and scream while standing on the deck in front of my apartment door, saying, "The man that you are screwing forgot his fucking underwear!"

"What underwear? What are you talking about? Nobody has been here!" I went to look around in my room and noticed a pair of underwear on the floor poking out from under my chair. *Wow!* I thought to myself. "Larry, I am not having sex with anyone, and nobody has been at my place."

Larry left my apartment in a frenzy, and I immediately drove over to Eduard's house to give him back his underwear and take back my emergency key from him. He denied that the underwear were his, but he seemed to have a problem looking me in the eye. These were his underwear, black Calvin Kleins that he had purchased when we went shopping together.

Long story short, Eduard did not want me to be around Larry, so he tried what he could to break things up. That's my friend Eduard! Little did I know the favor he was doing for me.

Larry would always do childish little things that he tried to play off later. At first I didn't even notice some of the things he said or I would just brush them off. I noticed that he started to get upset when other men would look at me when we were in public, or when they came over and talked to me. Sometimes girls would stop me and start a conversation about my clothes, and he didn't like that either. I never understood what the problem was.

A few weeks went by after we got back from Japan and he was calling me at the weirdest hours. It was almost as if he didn't want me to sleep. By now the late-night conversations were not fun like they used to be. He seemed to call just to upset and piss me off on purpose. I didn't have time for this nonsense.

One particular night he called during the wee hours of the morning. When I picked up the phone, I knew it was Larry. He would take deep breaths, blow in my ear, and then pause. That let me knew he was smoking that funny stuff.

"I know the reason you don't want to have sex with me is because you don't want to get pregnant and have a child that looks like me," he said.

I was floored that he would even suggest that. I said, "I'm in college right now. I'm not thinking about having nobody's baby! A baby and some schoolbooks. Dude, that's the last thing on my mind and I am not married" He continued to say more nasty things. I finally said good-bye. Between listening to him smoke and breathe in my ear, I didn't have time for his gibberish.

Larry told me once, "You're probably going to start aging really bad now." Mind you, I was only in my twenties. Another thing he said to me was, "You know, you're really not all that. I've seen prettier." Wow!

He would always try and make me feel like I was doing something wrong, when I knew I wasn't. He would say demeaning, degrading things to me and then always make an excuse for it afterward. "Aww, baby, you know I'm just kidding you. Hey, I wasn't serious, I just had a bad day." Once I asked him about his marital status, and he just smiled. "Well, you know, like the old saying goes, it's cheaper to keep her." When I asked him what he meant by that, he said he was just teasing me and laughed.

But there was no getting around the fact that he was angry whenever people paid attention to me. I couldn't help it if people wanted to come up and talk to me. I like to talk to people. I didn't understand his attitude. What I didn't realize at that time was just how jealous he was. I would soon find out.

We were talking about music one day, and Larry asked me who I liked to listen to. I told him I liked a lot of different music, but I admitted to him that I wasn't familiar with his group. I told him that I liked gospel, Al Green, Michael Jackson, Marvin Gaye and classical like Mozart But to me, my favorite artist was Prince. I wasn't really into Larry's group *"Cameo"* type of music which was Funk.

I told him that Eduard had gotten me the best front-row seat at Prince's concert. I was even asked to dance in one of his shows, and the best part was that I got to meet him. I didn't know that Larry was upset about that, but I found out later when Renee got in my face about it. "You should never have told him that," she said.

I didn't see what the big deal was, and I told Renee. I had met Prince awhile ago, long before I met Larry, and I was neither Larry's property nor his possession.

Have you ever heard of *Where's Waldo*? Well, that's Eduard in a lot of the stories of my life. Larry had a problem with it. He would say I was hooked on that man like a drug addict; he had me by the nose. I told Larry that wasn't true and to stop it! He would tell me, "I want you to stop seeing that man."

"Eduard is my friend, and my parents knew this man when they were kids in school. Eduard is family. You don't have to be blood to be family," I explained.

One night Larry called Eduard's house at one o'clock in the morning and said, "Hey man, this is Larry. We need to break bread and get to know each other because Tamiko talks about you all the time."

Eduard responded, "I got to go, man. I'm sleepy. We will talk again."

Larry started inviting me to some of his other shows. I was young and still a little naïve. He had the nerve to ask me to marry him. "Where's my ring?" I asked. He wanted to play these games. So he asked me to marry him and he said he'd find me the biggest, nicest, prettiest ring he could find.

He demanded to meet my mom. When that day came, she, too, wanted to know where my engagement ring was. He made an excuse about taking his time to find only the best for me. I could see from the doubtful expression on my mother's face that she wasn't buying it; however, she was cordial to him anyway.

I guess he was in a rush to show me that he wanted a serious relationship, but really all he was doing was making me believe that he was obviously nothing but lip service. The insult I really remember from that day was when he asked me if my mother's hair was "really that straight?" What was that all about?

He played these games, and as time passed, nothing changed. The next time he flew to Japan he called me at two in the morning and said, "I found a ring that would look gorgeous on your hand." But when he got back to town, there was no ring to be found. Then, he asked me to go with him on the mini-tour, which was three cities: Bay Area, Los Angeles, then Sacramento.

Once we reached the hotel room before the last show, I went into the bathroom to do my hair and makeup as he got ready in the other room. I asked him where I needed to go to see his show. I figured I'd take a car out there later, since he'd have to get to the place early for sound check. He walked out of the room without telling me anything, locking the door behind him. He just left me there. So I didn't go to that show. Honestly, his music is not my thing anyway and I was upset, so I didn't want to go anyway. The tour ended that night and we returned home.

Back at my apartment once again, Larry didn't call for two weeks. I had a chance to breathe and was happy with that. I tried to call him to let him know I was done with the bad treatment, but would you believe the phone number he gave me didn't work. But here is the strangest thing. I would get calls late at night from somebody who would just breathe on the phone. Gee, I wonder who that was. This was the 90s when we didn't have phone options like star 69 or caller ID.

Larry called me one day, and would you believe it was in the afternoon. I did mention those late-night breathing phone calls, but the answer from him is not worth repeating. It was the same old story, just a different day. He called me to talk about things we could do together and gave me several options. He brought up the idea of going out on a boat.

"I don't know about that," I said. "I used to be a pretty good swimmer before my accident."

Larry laughed, "Oh, so you mean you'd be easy to kill, huh?"

Of course, he was just teasing. But I pointed out that I wasn't okay with him saying it. Why would you say something like that? He told me that I was too uptight and just couldn't take a joke.

A few weeks later he was going away on a trip to play with his band—I think it was back to New York, flying out of San Francisco airport—and he needed someone to drop him off. Larry was very nice to me and asked me to take him to the airport. We were chatting, laughing, and having a good time, and everything seemed fine. When we got to the airport, a lot of people were unloading passengers and getting bags out of their cars. There was nowhere to pull over, so I had to circle the block, hoping to catch a spot as soon as someone pulled out. I told Larry, "I'm sorry. I have to go around again and come back. The guy is signaling me to move up."

Then Larry screamed at me, "If you don't let me the fuck out of this fuckin' car, I'm going to fuckin' tear this car up!"

I slammed on my brakes, stopping in the middle of the street. "Get out of my car!"

He got out of the car and pulled his bags out of my trunk. I got out of my car to make sure my things in the trunk stayed in place and told him, "You know what? I tried to be your friend, but I'm done!"

Larry laughed. And that was the end of any vestige of friendship we had.

From that time on, Renee would call, and kept bothering me. She said that Larry was asking for me and wanted to see me. This was a month after the airport scene. I couldn't figure out why he wanted to see me unless it was because he wanted to apologize for his bad behavior toward me. I told her I was done, I didn't want to be his friend anymore. I should have followed my first instinct and not gone to meet him—but I thought if he wanted to apologize, that would be a good thing. I am always open to forgiveness.

That night I was in the audience enjoying Larry's music with Renee. A gentleman came over and asked if he could buy me a drink. I told him, no, thank you, I was already with someone.

"Who?" he asked.

"The lead singer in the band," I told him.

"What? Really? Where do they get all these pretty women like you? Do they grow you on an island somewhere?"

I couldn't help but laugh. "No, I wasn't grown anywhere, but thank you for the compliment!"

He smiled and gave me a wink. "Well, you have a good night, miss."

Another guy came and said hello a few minutes later. But I told him the same thing, and he said a polite good-bye to me as well.

Meanwhile Larry, on stage, was so focused on what I was doing that he couldn't concentrate on his own act. I spoke to him after the show, and he was on another mental trip asking me if those men were my boyfriends. I said no, they had greeted me and offered me a drink. "I told them I was your guest and they left me alone." I didn't have time for this nonsense, so I left and went home.

Renee later informed me that Larry's son had banned me from coming to any more shows while his father was in town. I said, "Okay, I'm fine with that, but out of curiosity, what did I do this time?" She couldn't give me a sound answer but laughed so hard, telling me that the other night Larry had been running down the hallways at the hotel into the rooms of his band-mates, looking under their beds, asking, "Where's Tamiko? I know you're under there. Tamiko, you better come out!"

Renee laughed so hard that I started laughing too. I had been at home in my bed, a good hour away from the venue where he was playing. I told her when I had first met Larry, I asked if he did drugs. He said no, but I confronted him about it again and again, and he always said no or pretended he didn't understand what I was talking about. He played word games or pretended we hadn't talked about this topic before. The most recent time I had pressed the issue with him again, he had said, "I never said I didn't do drugs." I told Renee I would stay home, and Larry would hopefully figure out I hadn't been there whenever he came off of whatever he was smoking.

I went on with my life. Then one day Renee called again to tell me Larry wanted to talk to me. "For what?" I asked.

"He just wants to talk to you; you guys didn't end well. You can't come to the show, but he would like you to come and see him after the show at the Holiday Inn."

I said, "Really, Renee? Don't you think this is really tired now?"

Renee said, "He wants to talk to you, girl. You guys didn't end well."

Renee went on and on to convince me to pick her up and go talk to Larry because he really wanted to. I finally said, "Okay. I'll pick you up. What time?" I picked up Renee and we went to the after party at the inn. The place was packed with people. Come to find out the Holiday Inn was also having a class reunion there. Renee and I passed by the front desk and stood in the middle of the lobby waiting for some of the traffic around the elevators to clear so we could go up to Larry's room.

Then I heard someone scream, "You ugly bitch!" I knew Larry's voice, and I slowly turned around. I couldn't believe he had the nerve to call me an ugly bitch in front of sixty or eighty people at the hotel.

I turned around real slow. "Well ain't that the skillet calling the kettle black! Tell your mother I said hi," I replied.

Everyone said, "Ooohhh," and the room became quiet. They all waited to see what would happen next and which one of us would have the last word. The scene was so juvenile. As upset as he already was, he looked absolutely shocked that I had the nerve to speak up to him. It probably had never occurred to him that I would. He stood still and stared at me. I felt like we were in the twilight zone because everything seemed to be in slow motion. His hands were at his sides, but he curled them slowly into fists.

One man yelled out, "Man, she just put you in check," followed by other people's murmurs.

He then stomped toward me with a look of sheer fury in his eyes. I thought he was going to hit me, so I stood still and planted my feet. I was done running from bullies in my life and was determined that if he was going to do it, I was going to take it. He wasn't going to scare me off or force me to back down. I was done with that in my life. He was going to have to hit me in front of all the people in the lobby, and I was going to sue if he did. The way Larry was acting and looked at me, he was beyond angry with me. He walked up on me with this look on his face and hate in his eyes. There are no words.

He didn't put his hands on me, but he got so close to my face he could have kissed me as he rolled his neck from side to side like a snake while verbally assaulting and abusing me. That's how this story reminds me of *Sparkle*.

• • • •

Years passed, and in 2001 I was engaged to a wonderful man I was about to marry. Talking to Renee, she brought up the memory of Larry. "You two were like Beauty and the Beast. But," she chuckled, grinned, and told me, "oh, yes. Larry flew me to New York and he treated me like a queen." I asked her if they were dating. Renee responded, "Hell no, girl. That man is ugly!"

My friend Bernard laughed when I told him this story. "Now Tamiko, you realize that girl was just breaking her neck to tell you that."

A few years later in 2003, Renee called me up and asked if I wanted to go with her to a show to see a group of singers. I said, "Sure, why not?"

When Renee and I arrived at the event, we were in the back with the performers, and, oh my, Larry was there. He told me he had just bought a new house and that I should come and decorate it since I was an interior decorator. Larry put his hand up next to my wedding ring and said, "Look, our rings match. We could say we are married when you come out to my new house." He asked me to leave my husband for him because he didn't feel comfortable being around me since I was married to another man.

"I'm not cheating on my husband. I don't do things like that," I told him. "And why would I want to leave him for you?"

As I stood there listening to him talk to me, it hit me like a ton of bricks as I looked him straight in his face, and it just made me sick. Thinking back to our time together, he had been attracted to my beauty but also despised me for it. It made a lot of sense that Larry would feel more comfortable with Renee. She was as ugly as he was inside and out. He didn't have to worry about competition or attention from other men.

After that night, would you believe I started to get calls again from somebody who would just breathe into the phone? Gee, again I wonder who that was. I told my husband who I thought it was, and after too much of the breathing we changed our phone number.

I thought back to how Renee used to say little things to me in our conversations and how it seemed like Larry would mention things that had been part of the conversations I had with Renee. That is when my relationships with Larry and Renee started to make sense. These two people are two faced and were not my friends; they were jealous enough of me to want to hurt me. I mean, think about it. They would talk long distance to each other between California and New York just to talk about me. Wow! How can people be so petty? Where are the morals, values, and ethics in their character? Did they ever stop to think about Tamiko's feelings? They wanted to walk all over me, and I had done nothing wrong to them. Renee was playing both ends against the middle. The bricks kept hitting me. My mother was right! Renee was jealous and pretending to be my friend, but she was just using me for what she could get out of me. And it was obvious that she was using Larry, too.

Between Renee and me, I was always the one with the money and the car, and when she wanted to go somewhere, she'd call me. She knew people who had connections to get us in places; however, she never offered to split the costs because she never seemed to have any money when it came down to paying the bills. She would on occasion pull bank rolls out of her pockets and make sure I saw it. My reply to that would be, "So you can pay me back the money you owe me now?" Her reply was always that it was not her money. I would respond by asking why she was showing it to me. This problem had been going on for some time.

The next time I saw Renee, I asked her about the $150 she owed me, and she gave me twenty dollars back. Finally something. The next time we got together, I asked her for the remaining balance. She came up with a reason that she did not have to pay it. As I listened to her talk, telling me this ridiculous story, I saw her true colors come out. I realized she had stolen from me when I caught her in a lie. She promised she would pay me back. I learned her word meant nothing.

I also remembered other things Renee had done. One time she came to my apartment and I had a bag of makeup—foundation—I was throwing away. She asked if she could have it and stated, "I'll take this because we are the same color."

I told Renee, "No, we are not."

"Yes we are!" she said firmly. I was done with that topic, so I changed the subject.

A few days after that we were going somewhere and I picked her up from her house. That day I wore shorts and sandals. I rang the bell and when Renee answered the door, she looked me over from head to toe, staring at my pale white legs and feet with this look on her face. I thought this was really stupid how people get caught up in color.

I thought back to when my mother met Renee for the first time and said, "Tamiko, that girl is jealous of you." At the time I had brushed it off. I hate for my Mom for being right about these things! Looking back, I wished I would have left her alone and sat with my cousin at our own table and enjoyed the show. Regrets. But when you're young, you don't have the experience to know these things for yourself, and it's hard to take other people's word for it. And sometimes, when it's something negative, you hope your elders are wrong. I was done being friends with Renee.

Later, in 2003, my husband and I were flying out of the airport in Oakland, CA, to Vegas, NV, and we couldn't believe who was flying there too. I was allowed to enter the plane early because I am handicapped. Renee entered the plane and saw me sitting in my seat. She said, "Hi, Tamiko. How are you?" I looked her in the face and then turned my back to look out the window. I said nothing to her. I think she got it. To me she's yesterday's news.

What really made me wonder about Larry was how he could treat me the way he did and then think I would be willing to go rushing back to wanting to be his friend. Why would I drop my life to return to his abusive treatment, his outbursts, his paranoia, his put-downs, and his casual drug abuse? To believe I'd be willing to leave a happy marriage in order to go back to him for those head trips? He must have sold himself on the idea that he was much more important than me. He thought I didn't know my own worth.

It just shows that some people will always put their convenience before your feelings as a person or human being. As the Lord has stated, "Do unto others as you would have them do unto you." Because in the end you will reap what you sow.

UPDATE:

In today's culture people are more self absorbed than ever and live in a narcissistic manner, "You're the one who is wrong, I am always right" type of thinking. Now when something happens which is different than that, it is looked at as out of the ordinary. Something like that happened to me which I never expected to happen. When The Lord speaks, asking of me to "Be Still." I have learned to listen and do so.

My husband and I woke up earlier than normal and started our day. It was still an early Sunday morning as we met standing in the kitchen. I was leaning against the counter holding my cup of coffee looking over at my husband when I asked him "I know you can't catch up on sleep, but it's still early enough to where we can get something out of it and not possibly affect tonight's rest. Are you in for a nap?" Yes! I heard with excitement. Setting my coffee mug on the counter top, we then both laid our bowls, plates and silverware in the sink. We proceeded, marching to the bedroom and wandered off to the bathroom to clean our teeth. Sitting our toothbrushes back in the holder we caught each other looking over at our pillows on the bed and laughed. I looked back at the bed then shifted my eyes back at him "let's do this!" I said, as we giggled with smiles on our faces. Getting back in bed; I'm now snuggled up and tucked under the blankets as my head laid cozy on my pillow. I heard the sound of my husband sleeping already. How does he go to sleep so fast?......I ask myself.

I feel myself falling deep, floating into my dream. My body feels heavily as I'm sunk into a pile of feathers as I start to rest. I was almost there, knocking at the door. Next step for me REM. Exactly at 11:59 AM June 29, 2025 the phone rang. It snatched me out of my sleep, woke me. I jolted. I then sat up not fully awake yet. Leaning on my arms looking down at my pillow as I'm still hearing the loud jingling then looking over at the phone blinking with lights that's sitting on my nightstand. Still a little groggy looking over at the phone from the middle of the bed. My emotions had thoughts with a touch of a little irritation from wanting to sleep. Who is this? Do I hang up or do I speak? Scooting over to the edge of the bed my foot now poking out from under the sheets "burr" as I felt the uncomfortable coldness as the phone continued to ring I then picked it up while looking at the flashing name on the screen and not recognizing it. My eyes traveled over to the bright yellow talk button that I pushed down with my thumb answering the call, these words squeaking out of my mouth. "Hello, Yes, this is she".

As I'm now in this conversation conversing with supposedly a stranger so I thought. While doing so I wanted to keep the noise down so my husband could continue to sleep. While talking on the phone I rolled out of the bed and slid my tootsies into my slippers then grabbed my robe putting it on while in conversation. I'm sorry I don't recognize your voice. From the caller all I heard. Shocked as

I'm standing in the doorway with my hand hanging on the doorknob "The Lord kept telling me to find you, to reach out to you and make things right." As I'm now walking out of the bedroom closing the door behind me I'm hearing "I have been looking for you for 24 years; now I found you. I am sorry for hurting you. I am sorry for all I have done to you that was wrong. Please hear my apology and my prayer. Will you accept it?." My response "You mean to tell me that you have been looking for me for 24 years to apologize?" Yes! She said, I Replied "Yes, All is forgotten. I accept your apology. This is beautiful. Thank you!"

Corruption, It's a Sick Dilemma
It's Insane
People Need to Change

I Pray
I Cry Dear Lord for Forgiveness
As I Beg

The World Is Hurting
I See
I Hear
And I Look
Evil Is Here
It Walks Among Us

I Am Amazed
You Revealed Yourself to Me

I Have Been Chosen
To Hear Your Voice
And Learn a New Way

I Know
There Are No Buts
But Your Words
Should Be Cherished

Tamiko Powell

The Globe
Goes Around and Around
But Yesterday Never Left

We Must Move On
And Understand a Test
The Tumbleweeds Will Roll By
The Moon Breathes Another Day

When Will We Get It Right?
What Will It Take?

We Walk Among One Another
With Nothing but Hate

You Talk to Me
I Hear Your Voice
Oh Father
With Honor and Respect
I Surrender
I Bow Down
I Open My Heart

We Must All Question
Our Lifestyles
And
Praise Him
Choose Life
Enjoy the Natural Wonders
Of How the Moonlight
Kisses the Sea

Stop Being Selfish and Greedy
He Doesn't Like What He Sees
Oh Dear Lord
People Won't Listen to Me
How Do I Tell Them
That You Have Chosen Me?

My Eyes,
Ears Are Wide Open
You Have Spoken
The True Meaning
Of Your Words
That Have Fallen
From Your Mouth

An Exclamation Point
That This World Is Doing Wrong
People, You Know It As Well As I Do
We Have to Change
This Evil Song's Tune

You Sow What You Reap
You Reap What You Sow
His Faith
Is What You Need to Know

The Devil's Goal Is to Screw You
And Give You Three Things
He Loves to Do

Our Father Is the Only Faith
Praise Him; This Is the Only Way

Times Are Hard
In the Worst Ways
Our Free Will Is Worldly
In a Sick Way

Lord, My Heart Is Open
Speak Thru Me
Speak Thru Me
To Those Who Want to Be Free

I Don't Scare So Easily Anymore
I Have Learned to Know
My Father Has His Soldiers

It Took Me Awhile to Understand This
But I Know
That I Know
He Has No Time Limit
We Hurt One Another
Like There Is No Tomorrow

He Will Question You
In Due Time
On What You Did
To Your Sister or Your Brother

Justice Will Be Served
Hades May Be Given
Your Ticket Number

I Have Cried for Many, Many
Many Years
Disbelief
Not Knowing
My Father Truly Loves Me!

I Was Caught Up
In Head Trips
In What People Did
And Said to Me

Trying to Fit In
The World's Definitions
Of Its Way of Living

My Father Has Informed Me
As One of His Almighty Soldiers
Wrapped His Wings Around Me

I Am Safe to Know
My Father Is Taking Care of Me

He Tells Me
Believe in Me

All I Have to Do
Is Listen
And Listen
As He Talks
And Tells Me Things

Things I Didn't Understand
Are Now a New Level of Discipline

With Respect and Honor
My Footsteps
Will Follow
His Straight
And Narrow

Outcast I Am
I Am Not!
Misled By Man's Free Will
That Leads to Sorrow
Not Missing Out
On Anything At All

It's Your Choice
Choose Wisely
On His Wisdom
For a Better Tomorrow

Father's Strength
And Wisdom
Guards Me

But I'm Still Singled Out
Because
The World Has
A Heartbeat
It Functions on Lies
And Backed Up by Disgrace
-Interpretation-
Of a Box of Categories
We Use to Segregate

Stop Being Ungrateful
Sins Will Not Behoove You

Things
That My Father Has Done
No Man Can
Nor Will Ever Do

There Are Trials and Tribulations
That Are Set Before You
Why Do You Do
The Things
You Do?

I Tell You
There Are Things
That I Know

Father Has Told Me to Tell You So
Are You Willing
To Put the World Behind You?

Chapter 10

The Idiot

Watch out who you become friends with and who you date. Those closest to you have the ability to do the most harm.

I thought this man was a nice guy. It wasn't until later that I saw the other, darker side of his personality. We started out having a lot of fun together. He would help me with my homework sometimes. We'd go out on walks or catch a movie together. It didn't really matter what we did, we enjoyed each other's company. The cracks in his character weren't visible until we had already been around each other for a time, and it was too late by then.

I met this man in a class. His name was Kevin. At the time he told me his aspirations were to become a singer. We started to spend time together. One day he was at my apartment watching television in the other room. He told me, "I have an idea for you to be able to go on a mini vacation for free."

He asked to use my phone. Within a few days we were invited to New York to be on the Sally Jessy Raphael show. He had called and told the producers a story. He called them and pitched them a show idea. He said that he was in love with a woman, but he couldn't tell her about his feelings.

"Why can't you tell her?" the producer asked. "What's the problem?"

"Well, because she's my cousin."

I didn't know what exactly he told them until we were on the show. It was a complete fabrication; we weren't related at all.

After we arrived at the hotel, he decided that he wanted to have sex. I told him no. He got angry when I told him no, I wasn't interested. Since I was in the middle of unpacking, he took my things and threw them in the hallway. "You're not in control of everything," he told me. "I'm the one in control right now." Hotel staff members came up to see what was going on. When I told Kevin that I could just as well fly home by myself, he calmed down and started to act like he had some sense.

He was consumed with the most childish things. He despised the attention I would get to the point he would blame me for it. I thought it was odd but just wished that it would stop.

He saw me coming out of class one day. He stopped me to let me know he'd straightened his hair and wanted me to see it. He said he had done it for me. I wondered why. I had never said anything to him about his hair. I told him there was no need to do anything like that for me. He should just be comfortable being himself. He always had to talk about how white his skin was. I have never been a person who was interested in race or skin color or just sitting back and talking bad about people. Looking back at that time in my life, Kevin was apparently not happy with himself because he felt his soul was stuck in a black man's body. But as the saying goes—if I had only knew then what I know now.

The two of us eventually moved to North Hollywood. I had my own place, a cute little studio that I loved. I didn't know it then, but one of his friends, Anthony, lived in the same building, just down the hall from me.

One thing about Kevin was that he had a knack for getting himself into places. One day we were out together and he got us into Motown Records. We ended up talking to a man there; I think his name was Brian. He let us know that this was very unusual and he wouldn't talk to anyone without a producer. He told us that was the policy throughout the industry, and no record companies would deal with unsolicited queries from artists.

But somehow, he was talking to us.

"What do you do?" Brian asked.

"I sing, and I write," Kevin told him.

"I see. What about her?" Brian asked, nodding toward me.

Kevin answered him before I could. "Nothing."

"Now wait a minute!" I spoke up. "You know very well I sing. That's how I met you, in voice class."

Brian crossed his arms. "Well, man, why don't you write the music and let her sing it? She's got the look. We can always do something with a girls' group."

That afternoon I went back to my place. He was mad about the way things had gone at Motown, but there was nothing he could do about it. I went about the rest of the day without thinking much about it. I was preoccupied with things I had to do: running errands, taking care of laundry, the usual chores that needed catching up on at the end of the week.

I showered, went to bed at my regular time, and drifted off to sleep. I woke in the wee hours of the morning with the feeling that I was being watched. I was startled to find Kevin in my bedroom, leaning against the wall. He said something to me. I only remember telling him that I had an interview the next morning, and I asked if we could talk later. I assumed he would leave.

I pulled my blankets up to my chin. He pulled the blankets off of me, and I started kicking at him. "What are you doing? Stop!" I said. The lamp at my bedside fell to the floor, and some of the diamond-shaped crystals came off the body of the lamp. Kevin picked up the pieces of glass and threw them at me. The light fell at strange angles over his face, leaving his eyes lost in darkness. He pulled my phone out of the wall.

I then noticed he had a gun. Shoving it in my face, he told me, "Smell it. This is your death, bitch!"

He beat and raped me. There was little I could do against his size and strength and under the threat of his gun, but I did my best to get a few hits in.

"You ugly bitch," he growled. "Do you know I could kill you, blow your ugly mother fucking face off, put your body in the trunk of your car, drive you to the lake, and leave you there to rot?"

The assault went on from two in the morning until six o'clock a.m. At that time, he got up and turned the water on in the bathtub. He picked me up and threw me in it, trying to rinse the evidence of his crime from my body. When he ran down the hallway to his friend's apartment, I took a chance and ran for it. I made it downstairs to my car.

I drove to the Chevron gas station across the street and called 911. Every 911 call is recorded. I told the person on the line that I had just been battered and raped. I let them know that my attacker knew martial arts and he had a gun.

Five police officers arrived on the scene, all male. The man in charge had an attitude. When I told the main officer in charge that I had been raped, he wouldn't meet my eyes. With a sigh, he said, "All right, so I have to call over for a female officer to come look at you."

When she arrived, Officer Michesney got into the backseat of my car with me and I showed her the bruises on my body. She told me that this was ridiculous and the man involved obviously needed to be arrested. She instructed me to follow the police in my car back to the apartment building. I pulled up into my parking space. Once we were there, she told me to wait in the car.

Within a few minutes, she came over, gave me her business card, and told me that they had him. "We got him. I want you to go down to the police department and file charges against him."

The police had gone back to my apartment building, where they found him in the shower washing off the evidence. He was taken into custody.

I went to the police department as the officer had told me to do. I waited in the detective's office. She told me to sit down and tell her what happened. As I told her what happened, she interrupted me and stood up.

"Hold on. I am going to get a few other detectives that have been in the business for a while because they need to be in on this."

"Why?"

"I think they need to hear this."

She called in several male officers, five or more, who came into the room and sat down. Detective Karen Crawford told me to get on the floor and demonstrate because she couldn't figure out how he had put his dick in me.

She laughed. "Okay, Tamiko, explain to me how he put his dick in you, because I simply don't understand," she said, laughing.

"I was raped! Are you gonna take me to the hospital?" I asked her.

"What hospital are you with?" she asked.

I said, "I'm with Kaiser."

"Well then go to Kaiser and get treated there."

I went to Kaiser thinking that they would be able to treat me. I waited out in the waiting room, and eventually they brought me back into the examining room where I was given a drape to put on. When the doctor came in, I told him what had happened to me. The doctor told me that they didn't treat crime victims. He told me to stop and put my clothes back on. I could tell that he was upset that this had happened. He told me to go back to the detective or call the police department and find out from them where I should go to be treated. He said that in the interim I could not bathe, brush my teeth, comb my hair, or change my clothes until after a rape kit was collected.

I went home and called Detective Crawford's office. The secretary said the detective wasn't available to speak to me. When she asked what was wrong, I told her that I had been raped. She told me to go to the San Fernando Community Center.

Once there, I saw Dr. Michelle. She said we had to wait until the officer was present before doing the rape kit. A rape advocate was there waiting for me, but she left early because she had a flight.

After we waited an hour or so, the doctor told me we were going to go ahead and do the exam.

"I know you're tired and you want to go home and clean yourself," Dr. Michelle said. She tried calling those officers many times. But the police officers never showed. Dr. Michelle documented the entire incident, including all her phone calls, and took down my contact information.

Dr. Azen came into the room and took pictures of my bruises.

Dr. Michelle called the police again and again, but they didn't come to pick it up. . Dr. Michelle noted in the report that I could be reached at my cousin Valentina's address in Oakland, California.

Instead of picking up the kit, the police would later claim that there was no evidence and they couldn't find me.

Dr. Michelle said she had everything she needed from me and released me to go home. I went to IHOP to get something to eat and to figure out what I was going to do. I thought that I would be able to eat, but I was nauseous and exhausted. I had been given so many pills: something to prevent disease, another for birth control, and different medications for pain. I couldn't get down more than two bites of food and a few sips of water.

I called my cousin Valentina from my apartment. I asked her if I could stay with her for a little while. She said yes and asked how long it would take for me to get there. I let her know that I was driving, so I wasn't sure. She said that she would be waiting for me.

I hung up the phone and continued packing. I had a packing service help me get my things together so I could get out as quickly as possible.

Anthony, Kevin's friend from down the hall, called me on the phone, laughing. I held the phone and listened in shock as he told me how Kevin had told him that he planned to attack me, all the things he wanted to do to me, and how he liked to do it.

"Why would you call me to tell me this?" I demanded.

"Well, I told him not to go over to your apartment and do anything stupid. He came over here with his gun and all his stuff and asked me to stay here."

"Why didn't you call me? Why didn't you call the police? How come you didn't answer the door for the police?"

"I'm not getting involved in that." He laughed. "It's not a big deal."

I hung up the phone.

I approached Officer Michesney and told her that Anthony was still in his apartment.

"We can't just go in there and take the gun if he won't come to the door."

I was still packing when the phone rang again. This time, it was a collect call from Kevin. I denied that call and hung up. About five minutes later he called again and I hung up on him. Finally, on the third or fourth call, I asked him how he was able to keep calling me.

He said he was in someone's office at the police department, and they allowed him to call. Once he told me that, I told him to stop calling me and then hung up on him.

Four hours later, I was packing up the last of my things in the kitchen, and Kevin was back in my apartment. Somehow he had been released. I picked up two knives from my countertop.

"How did you get in here?" I screamed. "Get out of here! I'm calling the cops!"

"I know that your stuff is moved out of here, but you know, we can still fix this."

"Fix what, you crazy sick?" I screamed back.

A neighbor had heard my screaming and called the police, and an officer walked in just then.

"Did he touch you?" he asked.

I wish I had lied, but I didn't. The answer was, "This time, no."

The police officer slammed him into the wall. He pinned Kevin down so he couldn't move.

I hustled out with the last few bags I needed to get. The manager walked up.

"I'm done with this lease," I told her.

"I heard what happened," she said. "I'm sorry."

I drove from Los Angeles to Oakland—an eight-hour trip—without getting any sleep. I hadn't told my cousin what had happened. Once I got there I cleaned up and went to get a piece of bread and some more water. I was so exhausted but still trembling from the effects of adrenaline, anxious and unsettled.

Valentina's girlfriend came to visit around nine that morning. Valentina wanted to introduce me to her. I came out to the living room so we could talk. While I was sitting on the couch I was aware that the girl was looking at me, but I didn't pay any attention. After all, my cousin knew I wasn't gay. The only thing I could really focus on was the thought of finally getting some rest. I spoke to them for awhile to be cordial, said it was nice to meet her friend, but I told them both that I was tired and needed to get some sleep.

I went to the bedroom and laid down to get some sleep. I was expecting that the police were going to call me to say they had arrested Kevin. I barely got any rest at all before the phone rang. About thirty minutes after I laid down, Valentina called me from work. She said I had to get out of her house.

"I'm tired," I said. "Please, I need to rest. I've had a long drive and I don't have anywhere to go. What did I do?"

"I don't care," she retorted. "I want you out of my house before I get home."

I packed up my things and left.

I went to stay with my brother for a few days. After that I called my sister and ended up leaving California to go visit her in Germany. I also had a chance to go visit my other brother who was living in Germany as well. I was there for about two months, and it gave me some time to rest and recuperate, to get away from the trauma I had been through.

Meanwhile, Kevin was calling my mother's and brother's houses in California looking for me. When my mom told me what was going on, I told her I wasn't speaking to him anymore. The next time he called, my mom told him to stop calling. After that, she started to get anonymous calls where someone was breathing on the phone.

My sister came up with the idea to let Kevin know that I wasn't in California and that he should stop hounding my relatives. I sent him a postcard that said, "We're through. I've moved on with my life. Stop calling my family."

Once I came home, I was able to get a new job and a new apartment. I moved on. I wondered why Kevin wasn't in jail. This animal managed to find me, beat me, and rape me for a second time at The Villa's Apartments in San Ramon. They didn't catch him; he got away that time.

Officer Simpkins came out after this second assault. When I told her what happened, she ignored me and played with Pumpkin, my bunny rabbit, as if nothing I said mattered.

That woman didn't care! She didn't do her job. What happened to her oath to protect and serve? I showed her the sheets on the bed and the wash cloth in the bathroom, which should have had physical evidence on them, but she didn't care. He had punched holes in the wall, and the towel rack in the bathroom was bent. But she wasn't interested in any of that. She didn't take notes, pictures, or collect any of the evidence I showed her.

She put me in the back of her police car and took me to the hospital for the exam and rape kit.

When we got there, I was put in the exam room. The door was left open while the exam was being done. The curtain wasn't even drawn to allow me any privacy. Anyone who happened to walk by could see my body and what was being done to me.

I was angry with God because horrible things kept happening to me. Why was God allowing this to happen to me yet again? Did these people have no sense of compassion or humanity?

• • • •

When I was a kid, I learned that whenever I had a problem, I needed to climb the chain of command until I found someone able to help me.

So I spoke to District Attorney Lydia Bodin. She claimed she didn't handle these kinds of cases. I told her that I had her name because it was on the letter she sent me. I read her back the letter I had received with her signature at the bottom, but she denied it all. She claimed she had never dealt with this case. I was so angry that I was shaking.

"I am a human being! Treat me as such," I yelled. "Why are you doing me wrong? All I am asking for are my constitutional rights. You know I was hurt and you know from the evidence that man raped me! The police didn't escort me to the hospital nor did they pick up the rape kit. And they didn't arrest that man? What's going on?"

There was a moment of silence, and then paper shuffling in the background before Lydia responded. "I don't know what you're talking about, and it wasn't my case."

"Then why do I have a letter from your office with your name on it?" I demanded. "I'm going to sue you. You didn't do anything to protect me. I'll see you in court."

She laughed at me and I hung up on her.

I filed a suit in Los Angeles Superior Court against the Los Angeles Police Department for misconduct and negligence in the way my case was handled. Of course, the case went nowhere and was dismissed. The police are a fraternity—a brotherhood—who will do anything to protect those who fall under their ranks, even when it means lying to protect their own.

I tried to get back into my hobbies to take my mind off this mess. I was in class with my instructor one day. I don't know how this conversation came up, but I asked my instructor, Larkin, if he could talk to the police for me. I told him that I had been raped and beaten.

He knew Kevin and he mentioned the man had an anger management problem.

Larkin paused before answering. "No, I have known his mother for years, and if he did something wrong or illegal, I would speak. However, I don't believe he did anything wrong."

Are you kidding me? What's wrong with this world? What happened to morals, values, and ethics? Why was he condoning what Kevin did to me? That was the end of me going to that class. I felt like he was protecting Kevin.

A few weeks later, I received a phone call from Anthony, Kevin's friend who lived in the same apartment complex where I used to stay.

"You know, I always really liked you," he said. "I didn't want to talk to you while you were with Kevin, but I was wondering if maybe we could go out."

I was shocked. "Why would I want to go out with you? You know what he did to me, and you let him hide his gun in your house!"

"Look, Kevin beat and raped his wife, Lizzy. And she divorced him, but she got over it. Why can't you drop it and leave it alone and go out with me? I just want to take you out to a fancy restaurant," he snapped back. "I don't see why you can't do the same thing and get over it like Lizzy did."

"Are you stupid?" I replied. "No, she didn't get over it, because if she did, why did she divorce his dumb ass? The better question is why are you protecting and defending a man who beats and rapes women?"

I was floored that this man could say something like that to me. I hung up on him. To this day I still can't understand how he would ever think this was okay.

I called the news stations, trying to get people to hear me: the local affiliates for ABC, NBC, CBS, CNN, and newspaper agencies. I was trying to start a fire, force someone to respect my rights as a human being. It's sad, but Dr. Michelle said that even though she called them several times, they never showed. She put together the rape kit without them there. I told Detective Crawford that Dr. Michelle put my contact information on the front cover of the medical report: Valentina, cousin, along with the phone number where I was going to be staying when I left Los Angeles.

Dr. Azen wrote in the medical report that my statement matched the physical findings he documented: I was slapped, strangled, kicked, punched, knocked out, and raped.

When I spoke to Detective Crawford, she told me that Lydia Bodin was unable to press charges and have my attacker arrested. According to her, too much time had passed and they didn't have enough evidence. The police department also did not contact any of the witnesses, and in all that time they claimed they had no way to reach me.

I called and talked to Detective Crawford again. "What do you mean you had no way to reach me? I'm looking at the medical report right now. The phone number and name of where I was staying is on the front sheet of the report," I said.

"Well, you claimed you were beaten and raped," Detective Crawford said. "There wasn't enough evidence; all you had was a ripped ass and you are too black for them to see your bruises." I was appalled at what she said to me.

She repeated what she told me before, and said she couldn't help me. I was once again degraded because of my race, shamed as a woman, and disregarded as a human being.

I called the police department, looking for anyone who would speak with me about my case. I spoke to Officer Michesney, the woman who saw my bruises during the first attack.

"We know he raped you," Michesney said. "We just can't do anything about it."

That conversation came to an end. I called the police department in Los Angeles, again trying to get a copy of the report. I spoke to Officer Sue, and she told me rape is not a felony.

"Are you kidding me!" I slammed the phone down in anger. What was wrong with these people? The next day I called again and spoke to a lieutenant. She said that she didn't usually answer the phones, but she took the time to listen to my story. I explained that I had been trying to get the police report but the detective had told me it was against the law for me to have it.

"Who is the detective on your case?" the lieutenant asked.

"Detective Karen Crawford."

"Oh, I hate that fucking bitch! Hold on," she said, and I heard a shuffling of paperwork in the background. "Look, don't tell her you spoke to me. That woman is lying to you. I'm going to send you your police report. There's no reason you can't have it. This man has also done this to another woman, and I'm going to mail this to you too."

I called the hospital and spoke with a woman named Bennett who was able to send me my medical report. Up until then I had been denied that information too.

It just blows my mind. After that, I called the high end of the police department: the chief of police, then I called the inspector general and spoke to Rene Gardaya and made an appointment. I drove all the way out to downtown Los Angeles to meet with him.

"Something smells fishy," Rene told me. "I believe you need to get an attorney. I'm going to need a few days, but I am going to guide you through what you need to do."

Some other people came into the office, including his supervisor, and they asked Rene to leave the room. A woman came in soon after and told me that they were pulling Rene off the case because this is a case he would not be working on.

About a month later, I got a letter from the inspector general's office saying they had researched the matter and couldn't provide me any help. I can only believe that there was a cover-up going on, and that it had to do with the fact that Kevin's mother was supposedly a lieutenant in the San Francisco Police Department. But Kevin Smith is such a pathological liar, I can't say for sure what her rank was.

All I knew was that she was protecting this sick animal by having her friends, it was like a fraternity, in the police department stop everything I was trying to do to put him in jail.

I contacted the Office of Civil Rights, but they said they didn't handle these kinds of situations. I called internal affairs, the mayor of Los Angeles, Prepaid Legal Law enforcement, Nicole C. Bershon of the LA Police Commission, victims complaint and claims board. I called protection advocates, the ACLU, and the National Police

Accountability Project. Everyone had a different reason for why they couldn't or didn't want to take my case, but the one thing they agreed upon was the same: they were not able to help me.

• • • •

I got up one morning with the strangest feeling—a sensation of anxiety in the pit of my stomach, like something was about to happen. Something that wasn't good.

I wanted to go pick up a couple of things from the store. I wondered if I should walk. It seemed like a good idea. I had gained a little weight and thought that it would be better to get some exercise than bother taking my car. The store I wanted to go to was only a few blocks away, and I only needed a couple of things. I would get to stretch my legs and be back in no time at all. And even as I considered it, I told myself that I shouldn't go. Or I could take the car instead. It would only take a few minutes each way if I drove.

I'm stubborn by nature, and this negative feeling without explanation bothered me, this idea that I should drive instead of walk when I knew I could use some fresh air anyway. So I ignored the feeling. I pulled on some sweats, grabbed my keys and my purse, and went outside.

As soon as I was outdoors, the feeling was worse. I didn't know why. I started down the sidewalk. It was a normal morning, with no one in particular around. I passed by quiet houses with cars parked out front, leaves shaking on trees with the movement of the breeze.

When I turned the corner onto the street, I realized what was wrong. From the corner of my eye I saw a figure, a man I thought I recognized. I told myself it couldn't be him! I wanted so much to be mistaken, but Kevin stood there. I had moved several times since he had attacked me. I lived in a different city, but he had managed to track me down. I didn't know how he'd found me, but I was sure there could be only one reason for his presence: to finish up the job he had never completed. To kill me.

I pretended that I didn't see him and crossed the street. No sooner had I crossed, he followed and fell into step right behind me. I walked briskly but couldn't run. Because of my injuries I still walked with a cane. My goal was to reach the supermarket before he could lay hands on me. There were people there, potential witnesses, cameras. Maybe someone could help me. But if they couldn't, or wouldn't, there would be footage of what happened and what he did to me.

A black truck sped along the street, moving at least twice the speed limit. And at that moment, all I could think was that he was going to shove me in front of that car. How easy that would be for him. I prayed, "God, this is it. I'm about to come home."

And then I did something that surprised both of us. I stopped, turned around, and faced him. Kevin stopped in his tracks.

I stood for a moment and smiled at him.

When I turned back around, I didn't know if he continued after me, but when I got to the store he wasn't there anymore. I didn't know why he stopped or if he had doubled back to go wait for me at my house. After all, he knew where I lived and that I would come home eventually.

Besides being a pathological liar, he had a lot of other issues like hate, anger, and jealousy toward me as a woman, all falling under the umbrella of trying to control me. It was overwhelming. It was like occasionally the devil himself would vacation in this man's body. It was a whole other level of ugliness.

When I got back to my house, I called my husband and the police. The authorities couldn't find Kevin anywhere in the neighborhood. I called United Against Sexual Assault of Sonoma County Hotline. They let me know that the restraining order from before had expired and I would need to file for a new one. They tried to help me, but it was no use. Even though they showed the judge the police report detailing the injuries from the rape, the judge denied it. She claimed that Kevin hadn't done anything to me.

But where the law has not protected me, God has interceded. For years I wondered why it was that I turned around and smiled at this man who had brutally beaten and raped me. But our Father let me know why; it was something He made me do. The Holy Spirit was in the midst of the situation that day, and Kevin was made to understand that he was to leave me alone.

I have never seen or heard from him again.

Praise the Lord!

There Is a War On for Your Soul
Don't You Know

The Devil's Playin' a Game
To Harness Your Soul

God Is Alive and Well
He Is Here
Open Your Eyes
Your Mind
And You Will Know

I Believe I Will Win This Battle
When the White Horse Walks the Earth

It's On
The Battle's On

Every Day
The Devil's Showing His Signs
Through Your Greed, Selfishness, and Hurt

You Need to Make Right
Your Wrong
To Make Corrections
On This Earth

If You Won't
You Are Merely

Nothing More Than Dust
And You Will Reap What You Sow

The Lord Sent His Son
To Die for You
This Is Something
In History
I Thought You Knew

Remember and Know His Love
Love
Not for Separation of Race
Not Even for Religious Titles
Or Other Ways of Hateful Waste

Remembering the Word
As Your Shield to Guard
From Fears of Belief
Life Can Cause

I Believe in Him
The One and the Only
You Can't Survive
On Just Bread Alone
But the Words
Out of God's Mouth
Are What We Need to Know

I Look At This Box
And the News Is Harsh
I See, I See, I See
And I See
Fragments of Lost Hearts

So . . .
In the Mornings, Lord,
I Will Lift My Voice
And I Will Look Up

Putting the Bad Things behind Me
I Continue On with Hope

Remember
The Devil Roams About
Like a Lion Roaring in Fierce Hunger
Seeking Someone to Seize Upon
And Devour

Whomever Resists Steadfast in Faith
There Is a War On for Your Soul
If You Didn't Know

Chapter 11

The Legal Thief

The government forces you to prove your innocence when in fact they are required to prove your guilt before taking action against you. Bullies find it easier to operate on the basis of threats instead. When I got a bill from the IRS for $25,000, my friends thought my response was crazy. Every experience I've had, from the time I was a young lady until today, has formed who I am. I've had many adversaries and my share of headaches during my lifetime. And like many people, I have gotten fed up. That's why I was going to stand up to any bullying, even bullying by the IRS.

When I received this bill stating that I owed all this money, I was in disbelief. Who made this decision? There was no way I could have owed them that. I wrote them a letter saying that I had recently been in an accident that put me in a coma and that I did not need any more stress. I went on to tell them that I did not owe them any money. Furthermore, I told them I would sue them for intentional infliction of emotional distress, negligence, and misconduct. I received a letter back from them not long after, apologizing for what they had done to me. Their letter stated that bill was void.

I Want My Children to Call My Name
Only in Need, Praise, or Help
Not in Vain
It Hurts Me!

You Have Trouble(s) On Your Mind,
You're a Struggler
Society Has You Acting
As An Animal

A Victim of Things
You Do to Maintain

Trying to Survive
In This World
Without Me

Either Not Knowing
Or How to Believe

I Am Here
I Am Real
I Can Lift You Up

If You Choose to Believe
And Follow in Me

It's As Simple
As Your A, B, Cs

In Life
The Flesh Is Weak
It's Needy
It Stink Thinks

Has a Resistance of Peace
It Causes Pain
I Can't Believe

As I See
The Tears
From Each Set of Eyes
Running Down Cheeks
Why?

I Give You Everything
But You Deny
My Love
Each and Every Day

This Free Will
Has the Devil
Living Up to His Games
That He
Loves to Play

Around
And Around the World
Killing, Stealing,
And Destroying

Instead of You
In the Bed
Counting Sheep
You're Harming One Another
Over the Most
Ridiculous Things

It Shows Me
You Don't
Take Me
Seriously

Those Material Things
You Fight Over
That Help You
Puff Up
Your Chest
Make You Think
You're Better
Than Your Brethren

Do Belong to Me

When You Leave
Your Body
They Will Be Left There
For the People Behind
To Squander Over

Now . . .

Beauty
Is in the Eye
Of the Beholder

Reaping What You Sow
For the Good or Bad
Is a Real Thing

My Children
Believe in Me
Forgive
Turn
The Other Cheek
I'm Everywhere
See Me

Don't Lose Hope
Believing in Me
Or My Word

Who Are You

And Why
Are You Judging
One Another

As Though
You Have a Right To

When All of You
Are Born with Sin
Only I Can Judge Thee

Then
You Think
You Can Judge Me

I AM
The One and the Only
The Almighty
The Maker
Of Heaven and Earth
The Seen
And the Unseen

The Days Are Running

The Horns
Will Be Blowing

Choose Wisely

Chapter 12

Silver Coins

One of the things I have learned is that friendships are not always what you think they are. People put themselves and what they want ahead of doing what's right. Sooner or later, though, people will reveal their true character to you.

I went to a university in Pennsylvania, or as I called it, "The Big P." I met a woman who worked for the school named Andrea. I don't remember her exact title, but she was one of the people who helped get students registered for their classes. We ended up talking and becoming friends. She told me all kinds of personal things about her family and problems she had with them, and I listened to her. It seemed like she was going through a tough time and didn't know what she should do about what was going on between her parents or with her siblings.

One day I was going through my room and decided I wanted to reorganize. I had some clothes I wasn't using that I wanted to get rid of. I had one pile of clothes I was going to give to some relatives. As I was going through my things, I came across some costume jewelry I wasn't using anymore. And for whatever reason, I thought of Andrea. I called her and asked if she would like this bag of jewelry since I would probably end up tossing it if she didn't. She told me yes, she would love to have it.

I sent her the box through the mail, with a tracking number so I could make sure she received it. But after I had already sent it off, I realized I had dropped in one piece of jewelry that didn't belong: a heavy bracelet made of three sterling silver coins that were the size of silver dollars. All three coins were set into individually adjoined bezels with a closing clasp. It was probably only worth two hundred dollars or so, but as far as sentimental value, it was priceless. It was a gift from my dear friend Eduard.

I called Andrea and let her know that my bracelet had been accidentally packed into the box I sent her.

"Did you get it?" I asked.

"Sure, I have it. I'll send it back to you," Andrea told me. She asked for my address, which I gave her.

After that I continued to check the mail for a box. Several weeks passed. Weeks turned into months.

I called Andrea, and at first she wouldn't return my calls. When I finally got in touch with her, she said that she had gotten a transfer on her job and would soon be moving to Arizona. She apologized for the delay and said she would go ahead and mail it. Andrea stated, "My supervisor told me that I wasn't supposed to talk to you anymore, anyway."

Another two months passed without any further communication. I decided to call the school and left her a message asking her to please call me back or just mail me my bracelet. Nothing, no reply back. So I called the school and asked to speak to her manager.

I spoke with Andrea's supervisor and told her what had happened.

"Well, we have never had any problems with Andrea," she admitted. "But I have got to say, I am really surprised. This doesn't sound like something she would do. I'm sorry that this happened to you, but she shouldn't take anything from anyone at the school; we have a policy. I'll speak to her about returning your bracelet."

Some time passed and I spoke with Andrea's supervisor again. The supervisor stated that Andrea told them that she left the box back at her mother's place. Her mother had searched for it in the garage but couldn't find it.

Another month passed without any word from her, and I ended up calling her supervisor again. I told her that Andrea had said the supervisor had told her she could not be my friend and was not allowed to contact me.

"What?" the supervisor cried. I could hear the frustration in her voice. "We don't interfere in our employees' personal lives like that. I didn't tell her that and never would."

I got in contact with the police and told them the story. The officer I spoke to was kind and listened to me.

"Honestly, since she has moved now, it's really up to her to return your bracelet," he said. "But she shouldn't have stolen from you, she shouldn't have done that. If I was her, I would have just returned the entire box back to you."

I called her again.

"Would you stop harassing me!" Andrea said.

"Why won't you give back my bracelet?"

"I don't have it," she replied.

"Really? Don't play games with me. I have the tracking number, and you told me that you had the bracelet. Your mother can't find it because you have it."

"Please don't send someone down here," Andrea replied.

"I thought you were my friend," I told her.

"I know you did," she replied calmly.

"You're a liar and a thief," I continued. "I gave you a gift, but I did not give you that bracelet. You lied and you took what belonged to me because you have never had something that precious before so you're going to steal it from me! You are an ungrateful person. How can you wear something that you stole and be happy about it on your arm? You're a liar and a thief!"

"Will you stop calling me names?" she yelled.

"I'll stop calling you that when you stop doing it! You know God hears everything that's coming out of your mouth."

"Yes, and he knows what's coming out of yours too," she replied.

"Yes, Andrea, but I'm not the one who is lying and stealing. Thou shalt not lie, and thou shalt not steal. You will reap what you sow."

The sad thing is some people let their pride get in the way of doing what's right. She knew that she should have returned that bracelet back to me. But I never heard from her again.

Thinking back, God had told me that she would not return my bracelet and I had debated with Him. "Yes she will, because she is my friend." God was of course right, and I learned otherwise about her friendship. I should have listened.

When We Met

I Slid Down the Rabbit Hole
Getting Caught Up in All the Sins
Humans Had to Offer
And Did
The Devil Played Me for a Fool
So Many Times and Time Again

Until This One Day Came
My Heart Opened Up
I Saw Life
In a Different Way

Our Father Came to Me
And Relieved Me
From Sadness, Hate,
And Pain

That I Captured
And Bottled
And Held Tightly
In My Brain

I Carried
This Torture with Me
Every Day

All These Ugly Memories
Of How Man's "Society"
Mistreated Me

It Rephrased
My Way of Thinking
It Changed
My Way of Living
It Had Me Acting
And Doing Things
The Same Way

The Mirror's Reflection
Of Your Actions
Is Not
Who You Are!

Late One Night
As I Laid
In the Bed Sleeping
Curled in a Ball Dreaming

I Was Awakened
By Our Father's Visit
To Me
In My Bedroom
Just Told Me So

You Have Been Hurt
These Were the Words
That Were Whispered
From Our Lord's Mouth

I Knew
Who Was Speaking to Me
It Was a Knowing
I Cannot Explain

I Felt So Embarrassed of My Sins
I Could Not Ask Him to Forgive
I Knew and Know
Right from Wrong
But I Still Did Them

The Devil Had Me
Caught Up
And Entangled
Being Worldly

God, I Am So Sorry!
As My Voice Wiggled
With Tears in My Eyes

God Said to Me
Tamiko, I Know . . .

This
I Will Never Forget
His Voice
Was So Tender
And Softly Spoken

He Relieved Me
For a Moment
From All
Of This Pain
I Felt from Actions
In This Life
I Was Living

As I Laid There in Bed
He Told Me . . . Tamiko
This Is How You Will Feel
If You Follow Me

I Laid There and I Cried
God,
Look At What I Have Done
As Memories Rolled Through
My Mind
Like Pictures Being Flipped
In a Magazine

God, I Have Sinned!

Do You Not Know
What I Have Done?

God's Reply to Me:
I Know Everything
From Beginning to End
From
North, East, South and West

All is Forgiven
Pain No More
All of Your Sins
I Have Forgiven
What You Have Done
I Know Why
I Have Forgiven
All of Your Sins

This Feeling of Peace
Overwhelmed Me

With Excitement and Joy
Tears
Just Slid Down My Face
And Dropped
From My Eyes

As I Laid There

Now
On This Drenched,
Soggy, Wet Pillow

The Relief
Was So Amazing

As Our Conversation
Was Coming To
An End

God Said to Me
We Will Talk Again

I Said
God Bless You!
As He Laughed

I Just Caught
What I Said

As We Both Laughed

And I Said, Oh
I Can't Say That
Because
You Are You

WOW!

And We Both
Said Good-bye

This Is Now
A New Memory
Of When We Met
I Want To
Always
Carry with Me

Because Now
I Know He Is Real
He Is
With Me

Thank You!

Chapter 13

The Demon

I am so tired of being treated like less than a human being. I have had my basic rights as a person and as a citizen denied me. It seems to be a game to some that they can degrade another person for the color of their skin, their social status, or their sex. And that's only made worse when these acts are committed under the color of authority. I'm sharing this story with you for two reasons—first of all, because this behavior is wrong and is against the will of God. And second, because I won't be silenced and hide in disgrace because of what was done to me. Let it be known.

This case was filed in the San Francisco Superior Court and is now public information.

I went to Macy's Department store at the Stonestown Mall in Daly City, CA, for the first time in my life. I stood in line waiting to see some fashion jewelry in the case. When my turn arrived to get help from the sales clerk, I pointed to the jewelry set I wanted to see. She handed it to me. It wasn't what I thought so I gave it back to her.

"What do you think?" the clerk asked.

"Can you hold it for me?" I asked her.

"Sure. We can only hold it for three days. I can take your name and number, and in case someone else is interested in it, I will call you. If you want it, you can pay for it over the phone and I can mail it to you."

I gave her the information she asked for and took her business card. As I started to walk out of the store, I was attacked by Macy's security guards who grabbed me and punched me in the back of the neck. They shoved and kicked me.

"Stupid nigger, dumb nigger," one of them said. "No matter what color you niggers come in, you only know how to do one thing and that is steal."

Macy's guards patted me down and found nothing on me or in my purse or jacket pockets that was stolen. The guards took my license and accused me of being someone named Tamika Lawanda Powell. They kept pronouncing my name wrong. I kept telling them my name is Tamiko, not Tamika. I was held in the back room at Macy's and they would not let me leave. I overheard Macy's guards talking. "The officer coming to arrest her says he knows her," one of the guards said.

"Stop calling me that name! Why were these charges for shoplifting pressed on me when they did not find anything on me?"

Officer Charles C. Chan arrived with verbal threats and physical abuse. He told me he knew karate and could kick my ass. I was sitting down. Keep in mind that I was still handicapped from the motorcycle accident and the slip and fall I had at Fairmont hospital.

As he walked over to me, I told him I had done nothing wrong. The officer put his hands on me with the intentions to hurt me. He came up from behind me, grabbed me, and threw me over a desk and headfirst into the wall.

I screamed out, "I am handicapped, you're hurting me!"

As I fell to the ground, he picked me up and slammed me face first into the wall. I slid to the floor and Macy's guards screamed out, "That's what you get for stealing."

They moved out of the way to give the officer room to continue to abuse me. He threw me around like a rag doll, throwing me over chairs and sliding me over the desk, from wall to wall, floor to wall. I fell to the ground once again. As I lay there, the officer jumped on my back and handcuffed me so tight the cuffs cut into my skin. Then the officer hauled me up off the floor, laughing. He shoved, pushed, and forced me to walk out to his car.

I fell once again, stumbling. "I cannot walk fast like this. I am handicapped! My hips hurt."

I fell to the ground.

"Get up, get up!" he yelled. I lay there and couldn't move because I was in such pain. He pulled me across the concrete. The cloth on my jeans tore as I was dragged, leaving both my knees scraped and bloody.

Officer Charles C. Chan, badge number 1886, laughed the whole time he was doing this to me.

I was not arrested yet. I had the right by law to get up and leave, but this man brought me into the police station and handcuffed me to a bench.

"Don't go anywhere. I will be right back," he said, laughing.

I tried to talk to the other officers, but all they said was I could only talk to the officer dealing with me. They ignored me. When Officer Chan came back, I tried to talk to him again.

"I have done nothing wrong. You need to let me go. Look at my driver's license on the table." The officer told me no. So I told the officer to check my fingerprints. "Officer Chan told me the fingerprinting department was closed."

The officer continued to accuse me of shoplifting. He said that I lived around the corner from the mall and was a drug addict. I told him that none of those things were true.

"I live in Dublin, California. This was my first time at this mall."

I told the officer once again to look at my driver's license. "My name is Tamiko. Stop calling me Tamika."

Chan said he would be right back. When he returned, he squatted down beside my chair and got in my face and laughed again like this was all some kind of sick joke.

In his hand he held a file that was just far enough away that I could not read it. "You have a rap sheet a mile long," he said. "You're a drug user and a car thief. And you've stolen from the mall before."

"No, I do not do that! That is not true. I have never been in trouble with the law. Look at my driver's license on the table." He told me NO.

"The person you claim to be is dead and does not exist. I know who you are and I know what you did. You paid a doctor to bleach your skin, you dyed your hair, and you're wearing contacts so you don't look like a nigger anymore," Chan said. "Book her!" He then walked away.

I was not allowed to use the phone to call anyone to help me. I was booked, and bail was set at seventy thousand dollars. I was told that as part of procedure I would have to be strip searched. When I refused to take my clothes off, I was told that they would hold me down and spread my ass for me. I was strip searched many times as Officer Chan stood in the doorway and made jokes as he watched and laughed. "Look how ugly she is."

After being in jail for a couple hours, another officer came and took me over to see a doctor. When I was led into his office, the nurse told me to go into the back room to put on a gown. When I asked why, she responded that they needed to check to see if I was pregnant. At first I couldn't understand why they would take me to a doctor. That is when I remembered what Officer Charles C. Chan had said to me earlier. He looked right at me and asked if I was pregnant because, "Niggers shouldn't breed."

I looked at the doctor and nurse like they were crazy. I refused, and they led me back to my cell.

During my discharge from the police department for lack of evidence, an attorney who worked there came up to me and she told me, "If I were you, I would contact Oprah." I did, but my story was denied.

After I was released, my friend Eduard took me to see Dr. Tipkins-Hood in Oakland to be treated for the injuries I sustained.

This racially motivated abuse has left me with nightmares, memories I can't forget, post-traumatic stress, neck and back problems, and physical scars. I still see a doctor today to help alleviate the pain in my neck and back.

As soon as I was up to it, Eduard took me to the records department of the San Francisco Police Department. The plan was to file a petition to seal and destroy the arrest record against me. We spoke to the custodian of records in that department, a woman named Ms. Statser.

She pulled the records of Tamika Lawanda Powell. In the process of handling the file, she dropped some of the paperwork on the floor.

Tamika Lawanda Powell's picture fell out of the folder and Eduard picked the folder up off the floor. We looked at her and could not believe what we saw.

How had I been wrongfully accused of being this woman? Ms. Statser agreed that I didn't look anything like Tamika. She was at least four inches taller, had a much deeper complexion, and was frail to the point of looking sickly. There was no way anyone could mistake us for one another. It was like comparing Grace Jones to Mariah Carey.

I had one small victory. I later received a letter stating that the district attorney's office had granted my petition to have my arrest record sealed and destroyed.

My first instinct was to fight for representation. I wanted someone to acknowledge what I had gone through. I had been denied my civil rights and received despicable treatment from an officer of the law. Though I knew what needed to be done, getting help to hold the officer and his department accountable for what happened to me wouldn't be easy.

I contacted a company called All Legal Services and gave an attorney, Warren Habared, five hundred dollars as a retainer. He said he would be able to help me with my case. After some time passed and I didn't hear anything back from him, I drove to his office to find out what was going on. The secretary was there, and she told me that Habared had packed up his office and left; she added that a lot of other people were looking for him too. He'd taken his clients' money and closed up his business without a word to anyone.

I couldn't understand why an attorney would do such a thing. He took money from people in search of help. Not only had I been conned out of my money, I needed to start the process of finding a lawyer to take my case all over again.

I wrote a letter to the mayor of Manteca, California. I received a letter back stating that Habared was a scam artist. He didn't have a license to practice law and had never been an attorney. The mayor has now banned him from running any business in the state of California.

Meanwhile, there were ongoing events pertaining to my case against Officer Chan. Because of my complaint, he was being investigated by Pat Dalton from Internal Affairs. She had the nerve to call and send me a letter telling me this officer did not do anything wrong and hung up on me. I tried calling her back many times, but she refused to take any of my calls.

I filed complaints and contacted various people and agencies for help: Jackie Canon, Secretary of State; Office of Civil Rights in Washington, DC; California Assembly Patricia Wiggens (Bob Klose); State Senate Wesley Chesbro; Willie Brown Jr., mayor of San Francisco; the president of the United States; San Francisco Police Department Prentice E. Sanders; the office of the attorney general in Sacramento. I also filed a citizen's complaint form and a claim with Richard Marrett in San Francisco.

I contacted Senators and Congresswoman Barbara Boxer, Noreen Evans, and Diane Feinstein, but everyone in Congress that I reached out to told me the case was outside of their jurisdiction.

The problem was that I couldn't find an attorney who was willing to go after the police department for misconduct. What I was told was that no one wanted to be involved in a lawsuit against a public entity. Attorneys flatly refuse to sue a police department and would not provide any legal advice. I called the ACLU and was told that while they do handle class action lawsuits, they didn't handle cases for individuals against the police.

My search for another attorney was disappointing. I talked to one attorney who said he would see what he could do to help me if I was able to pull a hundred thousand dollars' worth of equity from my house. Some quoted me six hundred dollars an hour. One had the gall to ask me for a twenty thousand dollar retainer up front. I was frustrated. I didn't have that kind of money or the time to drive around speaking to lawyers. Some of them just wanted to see what I looked like because of the argument of the case. I was tired of running up and down the state only for them to say they couldn't assist me after all. They argued that the case yielded too much work with no guarantee of any award.

I called a division of the NAACP in Santa Rosa, and they told me that the reason I couldn't find help was because I was a nobody!

I went back to the San Francisco Bar Association and was told by the manager that no attorneys there would go against a public entity. Another excuse I received from attorneys was that they wouldn't take a case if someone else had started working on it, even though I told them I hadn't found anyone to help me.

My doctor recommended me to Michael Finney. When I spoke to the receptionist in his office, she told me that I was lying because police officers didn't do things like that. I can only wonder what she thinks now when she turns on the news and sees multiple accounts of racially motivated police brutality.

I went to the NAACP and spoke to Dan Daniels about my case in San Francisco. At first he was excited about it. He told my husband and me that he had fought seventeen cases against the police department and won sixteen of them.

I stood in his office with my husband, who is white. I am mixed. Mrs. Daniels came in his office and looked at me, and then at the two of us. I had a weird feeling then that this woman didn't approve of what she saw.

Dan Daniels introduced his wife to my husband and me, excited about helping me with my case. Mrs. Daniels pulled her husband out into the hallway. The next thing I knew Dan Daniels came back in the room. Mr. Daniels said somebody else was going to call us. He would not be working with us anymore on this case.

I was shocked that even at the NAACP I had to deal with racism. That woman didn't like that we were an interracial couple and she didn't want her husband to work on our case. Again, I received no help whatsoever. They would not even look at the case.

Al Sharpton refused to look at the case. I contacted Jesse Jackson—that was a joke. I even went to local media channels 2,4,5,7, CNN, and all newspaper agencies to talk about how I had been abused by Officer Chan, but they would not even entertain a meeting.

I did continue looking with hope to find a lawyer while I stood in court pro per—meaning that I represented myself without an attorney—scared to death and not knowing what I was doing. But I felt as long as I told the truth, everything would be fine. As time went on, still searching for an attorney, I would still hear, "I'm sorry, I can't help you. Good luck with your case."

I was losing sleep, losing weight, and stressing out. What was I supposed to do? Oh God, help me!

To this day, I still continue to work toward receiving the justice that is due me in this case. God's grace has brought me this far, and I will continue to fight this battle. Officer Chan abused me and disregarded my rights as a woman. Unfortunately I wasn't able to retain an attorney, so I filed this case myself way past the statutes almost two years in the San Francisco Superior Court.

I went to every hearing while the defendants most of the time didn't show up, but the court in a way took care of me and didn't throw my case out. The defendants tried to demur and dismiss my case, they tried everything they could think of, but the court would not close my case.

I finally made it to mediation. I thought the nightmare was coming to an end. When my husband and I walked in, we let the person at the front desk know that I had arrived for mediation for the case of Powell vs. San Francisco Police et al. We were escorted into the mediation room. A representative from the NAACP was present named Mrs. Buford. She told me not to mention that she was there from the NAACP. A male from the NAACP was there as well, but he didn't want to be involved in the case at all.

I also waited for two more witnesses: Eduard and a woman from the San Francisco Court Records Department. This was the same woman from the records department who had seen my picture and verified that I was not the person they accused me of being. When we entered the room, the defendants sat at the other end of the table.

The mediator, Angela Bradstreet, asked what I wanted.

I asked for a monetary settlement.

"You don't deserve any settlement. So what that you were racially picked on?" Bradstreet replied.

"Well, the San Francisco Superior Court believes that I do; that's why we're here," I said.

Angela got upset. She walked over to the defendant's side of the table, picked up a paper, and shook it at me.

Someone knocked on the door. A woman came in and said that two of my witnesses had arrived.

Angela screamed, "No more witnesses in this room!"

I went out to tell Eduard and the lady from the records department that they weren't allowed to come in. They left and I returned to the room.

Angela Bradstreet shook a paper in front of me and slammed it down on the table in front of me. "You're not going to leave here without signing this. If you don't sign this, I'm going to place a lien against your disability checks. And because that's not enough money, and since you just got married, we will now file a lien against your husband's paychecks, his house, and his cars." She laughed. "That's not a good way to start a new marriage. So where will you sleep, and how will you eat Tamiko?" she chuckled.

After I signed the papers under duress, the indignation continued. She yelled, "If you go out and tell anybody what happened here, and I hear about it, I will sue you a thousand dollars per person."

Ms. Buford called me on the phone the next day and informed me that I should file an order to rescind my signature, so I did.

I went to a hearing that was held at the San Francisco Superior Court regarding the motion to rescind. Judge Goldsmith called my name. I stated my name, but before I could say anything, he said, "If you had an attorney, you wouldn't have signed . . . Next!"

The following day I pulled out the phone book in a panic in the hope of finding an attorney that would listen to me, give me guidance, and hopefully be willing to take the case on.

After making numerous calls I finally reached an attorney at a San Francisco law firm who would listen to me. I explained the case to her and she said, "Let me tell you some of the things she did wrong: number one, the defendants cannot be in the same room as you; number two, she cannot deny you your witnesses to the case; and number three, she cannot threaten your livelihood to force you to sign the dismissal."

This attorney unfortunately could not represent me because this type of case is not what she handled.

I filed another motion in the San Francisco Superior Court to set aside the dismissal of my case due to fraud upon the court. Judge Quidachay called my name and immediately denied my request. I attempted to argue my case about there not being any statutes of limitation for fraud upon the court, but he cut me short and told me to get out of his courtroom.

Time passed.

One day my husband and I were driving to breakfast. He ended up taking a different route than usual to get there. We passed a building that had a banner out front that said LDA for You. I took down the number and called the company the next day. I spoke with the owner,

Mr. Voller. He looked on his computer for some information. Within five minutes, he found what he was looking for, and turned the computer screen toward me so I could see it for myself. He pointed it out to me that they broke the law and that there were no statutes for fraud upon the court. I filed the case in the San Francisco Federal Court: Powell vs. Bradstreet et al., and the judge had assigned my case to magistrate Judge Jacqueline Scott Corley. I received a letter from the court asking if I wanted a magistrate judge or a judge. I wanted a judge that would come with a jury so my case could be heard.

In the process, Judge Corley filed a motion to dismiss the case. I filed an answer to her motion.

After that, unfortunately Judge Charles R. Breyer dismissed the case and had it pulled from the docket without allowing me to have a say. His statement was that he felt that none of the judges in the case had done anything wrong.

I believe this is a case of cronyism, and friends covering each other's backs.

If my case were heard, it wouldn't have been so easy to sweep this incident under the rug.

"Four Quarters"

We Walk Around
Looking Down
Not on the Ground
But on People
Where Did This Come From?
You Think You're Better
Chastising and Degrading
Just Being Ugly
People with the Pitter Patter
Of Ignorance, That Choreograph Their Life with It
Where Is the Philosophy
That Being Ugly Is Right
Contemptuous Treatment, Indignity
To Another Person's Life
Go Find Yourself in Christ

You Gotta Know Who You Is
'Cause This Ain't Where It Is in Life

Life Is Short
It's in Four Quarters

Know This
Before You Leave

It's Senseless to Believe
That Lies Are Not Evil

You See and You Do
Don't Think It Won't Be
Brought Back upon You

You Got to Know Who You Is
So Know This
Believe in This

He Sent His Only Son
And His Name
Is Jesus Christ

Our Father Walks upon Us
Do You See Him

Do You Even Think of Him
He Sees and Knows Everything from Beginning to End
Do You Only Desire Your Greed
Your Selfishness, Unnecessary
Of the Things

You Think You Need

He Knows It's Overwhelming
In This Sinful World We Live In
Your Free Will Can Be Misleading

You Need Help; Call Upon Him
Be Humble
Just Two Knees Down
And An Honest Thankful Praise Away
To Start a New Beginning

You May Not Understand
The So Many Things
That Have Been Written
It's All About Belief
In the Sincere Love of His Commitment

In This Sad World War Zone
We Fight to Live In
Pandora's Box Awaiting
For Another Fool to Lift Her Lid

But Know This . . . Hope Is the Only Way to Live
For Each Day That You're Walkin' 'n' Breathin'
You're Living with Yours or Someone Else's Worst Sin

To Open Your Eyes Is Understanding

Peace Is Believing
Knowing That with Him
No Fear Is in His Way of Living

I AM
That He Says to Me
All That You See
From Beyond Your Imagination
No Limits Exist with Me
You Must Strengthen
Your Belief in Me

A New Understanding from Enlightenment
From An Epiphany
Twice It's Been Told
Now I've Just Learned
How to Behold My Story

Chapter 14

The Awakening

I was in bed one morning and had a feeling that there was a presence in my room. I curled up in bed hiding under the sheets and blankets like a child is scared of a monster in a horror movie. Covering my face taking peaks while pulling the sheets down a few inches to see as I was searching for HIM in my room as I laid on my left side then pulling them back up while I'm talking to HIM. Screaming where were you? I waited for you ! His aura filled up the space, and though I couldn't see I knew exactly who it was. I heard the reply "Tamiko, Tamiko, Tamiko so calmly with no sense of anger or change in tone. But so sweet with compassion. My name was said many times as the pressure of His aura filled up the room. I was overcome with emotion. I thought of my life, all the things I had been through, and the people who had wronged me. I remembered what I had been taught as a child: that God loves us and protects those who believe in Him. I could only think of one question that I needed to ask Him. "I waited for you. Where were you?" I asked HIM again

"Tamiko," He repeated my name softly. I didn't have anything else to say. I only wanted to ask Him that question. It had been in my heart for so long. It was the manifestation of the bitterness and anger that remained in my heart, fused with the memories of being hurt and abused over the years.

He said my name several more times. And then He said, "You're not ready."

He was gone just as quickly as he came. And I would not hear from Him again for a long while.

• • • •

A few years passed. Life moved on, and I had moved into another house. I had been there only a few months when He came to me again in my sleep. I was awoken again because of the omnipresence I felt in the room.

He said, "Tamiko, everything you have done I have forgiven."

"God, you don't know what I have done," I said. For so long people had treated me cruelly, and I lashed out in kind. The world had hardened me.

"I know what you did, and I know why you did it," He told me.

"But God, I have done things, and I am ashamed."

"All has been forgiven," He continued. "I know everything from beginning to end."

He took everything away from me in that instant: all the anger, pain, and anxiety from everything was wiped away from me as if it had never existed.

I just laid there and cried as His peace washed over me. It was a feeling like I had never felt or had before, a peace beyond my understanding or ability to communicate. This was His peace that He gave me so I would be able to understand the promise of being completed by Him.

As our conversation came to an end, God told me when I come home that all of the havoc that was brought upon my life I would not remember, but for now there was a reason.

The next morning, I got out of bed, brushed my teeth, washed my face, and grabbed my robe. I was walking to the kitchen and putting on my robe with my mind set on getting my precious cup of coffee when I heard His voice that stopped me in my tracks. He had come to see me again, at the time I least expected.

"Can you not walk on your own?" He asked.

"Yes," I replied.

"Can you not think on your own?" He asked.

"Yes," I said.

"Do you not have a roof over your head?" He asked.

"Yes," I said. "Oh God, I am so sorry. I never thought nor looked at it that way." I always remembered the negative that came from my accident, never the positives that came out of it.

"I was there for you. I held you, Tamiko."

God said, "I have something I would like to ask of you."

"What?" I asked as I stood in the living room looking out the window.

"I want you to preach my Word."

"I don't know, I don't think I could do that," I told Him.

"You were chosen before you were born."

I shook my head. "No, why don't you pick someone else? I'm nobody. I don't have any money. I'm just a woman. No one will listen to me. Why don't you choose someone that people would listen to?"

"No," He said. "I don't want someone else. I want you. You have the holy heart."

"No one is going to listen to me, God."

We debated about this, but I told Him I would think about it.

The next day Jesus spoke to me. I was in my bedroom late one afternoon.

"You will go through the same things that I have been through, but you will not be crucified."

"I don't know if I can do this. I am not you."

He told me, "Trust in what my father tells you."

"Okay, I understand," I told him. "When I'm talking, how should I ask—for you or your Father?"

He said. "The Father and I are as one."

There was a knowledge that I was given that let me know the world is coming to an end.

I asked Him when this would happen. Jesus replied, "No one knows, not even I, and I am His son."

"What can I do to fix it?"

"Nothing," He replied.

With those words He was gone. I sat on my bed, staring into space for a while. I didn't know what to do. I was overwhelmed. What had happened? Was this real? I asked myself.

Days later I had a visit from the leader of all angels, the archangel Michael who leads the army of God. He held me in his wings and lifted me up, giving me a knowing that he is my warrior and would protect me. I was in awe that he came to see me and over the security I felt in his arms. As he put me down, I thought about what Jesus said: "Trust in what my Father tells you." I thought about all the things I was told and came to a conclusion on my decision.

Some time passed and I had not heard anything else from God. I had thought seriously of what was being asked of me and finally accepted that this was real, and then . . . nothing.

As more days of silence went by, I realized that maybe I should contact Him. I called upon God and He acknowledged me. I told Him that I was honored by what He asked of me and I would speak His Word. God also asked me to call him Father because calling him "God" kept us at a distance.

After this visit, there was a silence between us for a couple of weeks. Doubt started to creep into my mind, and I wondered again if any of this had happened at all.

Finally one night Father came to me, and told me to get up and write down messages of what I am to tell the people. He has continued to wake me up at night with these messages but I was told that I could not put them in this book.

Whenever I didn't understand what He was trying to explain to me, He pointed me toward things that would show me the same information in a different way. One day I turned on the television to just get some noise in the house. The television turned on, and the channel was set to a preacher named Joyce Meyer. I had never heard of this preacher and honestly cannot explain how the television was set to that channel, as I have never watched that channel before. I sat and listened to Joyce Meyer as she preached about the very subject my Father had just spoken to me about the other day and left me with questions. Her sermon clarified my questions.

I am not a church-going person and would definitely not be called a "Bible thumper"; however, both my husband and I were raised

Catholic, so I had been married to my husband in the local church by Father Denis, and I had gone to Father Denis in the past for counseling because of his compassion and understanding. I told Father Denis what the Lord had told me about the end of the world and my discussion with Jesus about the ending. He was thrilled to hear what I had to say. He was excited about what I experienced and showed me his sermon telling me that's exactly what he had spoken about the other day in mass. Pointing out how he had spoken on the very thing God had revealed to me. I asked him how all of this could be happening to me. I told Father Denis that I had told God I was a nobody, I have no money and I am just a woman.

Father Denis listened to me and pointed out a lot of other people who had been called by God. Father Denis said, "Look at Joan of Arc. She was a humble woman, without power or money, but she, too, was called by God. So why not you?"

Even though I believed what was happening, there is just a sense of awe in having been communicated with by God, having felt His presence. Looking back, I believe I was seeking out comfort and confirmation. Most importantly, I was trying to decide how best to share the message I was given.

I sent a letter to the bishop of the diocese. What I received back was a coldly worded form letter that didn't relate to anything I had written to him. It basically said I needed to keep myself encouraged and not lose my belief in God. I was proclaiming faith in a miracle, but they didn't bother to even reply to me about it.

Then one night the Devil came to see me.

The WORD - There Is No Other Way

He came while I was sleeping and showed me how my body had bounced around on the concrete like a ping-pong ball during the accident. "Where was God? Why did He let this happen to you? Where was He if He loved you so much?"

Father told me to control my thoughts and to not doubt my faith in Him. He said He had been there for me when the accident happened; it was His love that had protected me. He told me He held me.

I finally gave in to the Lord. I let go of my anger and embraced Him in my heart. How could I not now that I had learned the truth? This was my Father, and I wasn't going to let the things that happened to me separate us from each other anymore.

Later, the Devil told me that he hated me.

I snickered and replied, "I hate you too. Now get away from me."

As Father continued to teach me the Word, I had questions and concerns. He would tell me every day just to "believe in me." As time went on, it started to get a little easier in understanding. He began to change my perspective(s) about myself and the world around me. He instructed that if people tried to mistreat me, I wasn't to worry about it. He said that I should look at them as little children who didn't know what they were doing. "Vengeance is mine," Father told me. Being told this and now knowing this has helped me let go of the bitterness over the years, the ugly, hurtful things done to me in the past. I began to understand that other people's cruelty toward me had little to do with my being. I didn't have to let the past keep me in a place of suffering.

Meanwhile, I started to look into ways to spread the message.

I thought about billboards. I got in touch with a company and found out how much it cost. And another problem was that the signs would only be local. If I had a sign placed in a larger city, the price increased exponentially. I was also warned that certain topics were best not to be advertised in this way. Anything controversial was to be avoided. It became clear that this was not going to be a medium I was able to use. Trying to decide the best way to share the message I was given, I started to stress myself out on what to do and how to do it; to get his word out there, nothing seemed to work. Then my Father taught me to "Be Still". I learned how to wait for His word of guidance.

Some years passed, and one day would you believe while I was cruising the Internet to look at my emails, He put this book company up on my computer.

I spoke to Father, "Is this what you would like me to do?" And here we are today. It gave me space to talk about the Lord and also about my life, and a book goes everywhere. I want to be very honest with you here. I am a private person and never felt that what happened in my life was of anyone's business and should not be exploited; however, the only way to explain where I was in relation to where I am, I am using the instances in my life so that people can understand in how we treat one another, as Father has told me, that no one is better than anyone. No matter what we go through, there is redemption in the Lord, if only we are willing to go to Him.

God has already sent us His only begotten Son to lead us to salvation. No, we did not want to follow Him. Our free will was a blessing, but yet a curse. We must mind that His death washed away our sins. Wake up, sleepyheads, the Lord is near. Every man will bow down before

God our Father and give an account for his life. In other words, you will reap what you sow.

Now is the time that you must make a choice. You are not being forced. You have free will; you are not God's puppet. The Ten Commandments were to give you guidance and protect you from yourself, but yet we live in a worldly manner. Seeing the sins we live every day truly makes this world the devil's playground. The stories I have told you are true, hurtful, and very sad. They are just some of the examples of what people do and what people have done to me. The message of this story is to NOW tell the beauty that came from my heartache and pain. I lost my way and was mad at God our Father. He saved me without me knowing it.

I am here to tell you now that I am a messenger, and it is your choice to listen to me. Our Father has spoken and shown himself to me. I have been chosen and told to tell His Word to the world. Now once you've received it, it's up to you to figure out what to do with it.

It doesn't matter what brings a person; what matters is what a person leaves with. If you want to know the message our Father asked me to write down and tell you, ask me . . . Ask me.

www.ingramcontent.com/pod-product-compliance
Lightning Source LLC
Chambersburg PA
CBHW061645040426
42446CB00010B/1592